Nachricht
Die Menschen des Prometheus
SONATE
pour le Piano Forte
à Madame la Comtesse Thérèse de Brunswick
PAR
L. v. Beethoven.
REPERTOIRE
des
Clavecinistes
SINFONIA EROICA
Luigi van Beethoven
AVVISO
UOMINI DI PROMETEO
GRANDE SONATE
pour le Clavecin ou Forte-Piano
CHARLES de LICHNOWSKY
Louis van Beethoven
SIX
QUATUORS
LOUIS van BEETHOVEN
Sinfonie
mit Schluss-Chor über Schillers Ode: An die Freude
SEINER MAJESTAET dem KÖNIG von PREUSSEN
FRIEDRICH WILHELM III.
Ludwig van Beethoven
OUVERTURE
Leonora
N.3
Beethoven
TROIS TRIOS
Pour le Piano-Forte
Violon, et Violoncelle
CHARLES de LICHNOWSKY
LOUIS van BEETHOVEN
Oeuvre 1
SONATE
pour le Piano Forte
LOUIS DE BEETHOVEN
OUVERTURE
Leonore
Pianoforte
BEETHOVEN
Grande
Simphonie
2 Violons, Viole
Violoncelle et Basse
2 Flûtes, 2 Obois, 2 Cors
2 Bassons, 2 Clarinettes
2 Trompettes et Timbales
Louis van Beethoven
VIERTES
CONCERT
für das Pianoforte
Rudolph von Oesterreich
SINFONIE
Louis van Beethoven
Partition
OUVERTURE
Fidelio
L. v. Beethoven
PARTITION
Troisième
QUATUOR
pour 2 Violons, Alto et Violoncelle
Louis van Beethoven
DEUX
SONATES
Pour le Piano Forte
Composées par
Louis van Beethoven
Eine grosse musikalische Akademie
Der Anfang ist um 7 Uhr.

CURTIS INTERNATIONAL

PORTRAITS OF GREATNESS

•

General Editor
Enzo Orlandi

Text by
Gino Pugnetti

Translator
Laila Pauk

Published by
ARNOLDO MONDADORI EDITORE
and
THE CURTIS PUBLISHING COMPANY

THE LIFE & TIMES OF BEETHOVEN

CURTIS BOOKS

A division of

The Curtis Publishing Company

Philadelphia • New York

A RELUCTANT PUPIL

The family of Ludwig van Beethoven came from Malines in Flanders. They did not have an aristocratic background. The family tree shows that the last generations do not even include wealthy bourgeois. A certain William van Beethoven is a wine merchant in Belgium, and his son, Eric Abelard, is a tailor. But the son of the latter, Ludwig by name, takes up a musical career. He will be the grandfather of the great Beethoven.

Grandfather Ludwig played an important role in Beethoven's life. We can assume that his grandson inherited his musical inclinations, and it is certain that he left a lasting impression on the personality of the boy who admired him. Grandfather Ludwig had pursued a distinguished career as a musician. In 1730 he was chorister of the Chapter Sanctum Sanctorum in Louvain, then choir conductor, and "Musicus" of the Court. Finally, moving to Bonn, he became *Kapellmeister* by appointment of the Prince Max Friedrich. His wife, Maria Josepha Poll, was a heavy drinker, who had to be confined to a nursing home. This malady was inherited by her son Johann, father of the great Ludwig.

Beethoven's father was also a musician. A tenor at the Court of Bonn, he was bad-tempered and mentally unbalanced. But he was quick to recognize that little Ludwig possessed an exceptional aptitude for music. This drunkard of a father was Ludwig's first music teacher. His methods were harsh and often senseless. He compelled his son to practice for hours at the harpsichord. When he returned home drunk late at night, he would pull the child out of bed and have him practice until dawn. Ludwig confessed later that, exposed to the repressive methods of his father, he had often thought of giving up the study of music.

In the archives in Malines, an important religious community in Flanders, the Beethovens are described as being of Belgian extraction. The family tree can be traced back, with certainty, to the end of the sixteenth century. Extreme left: the cathedral of Saint Rambold in Malines, where Ludwig van Beethoven's great-grandparents were married. Malines was called "the city of churches." Its cathedral is still famous, and houses a Crucifixion *by Van Dyck. In this church, Beethoven's grandfather (illustration at left) began his musical career as a member of the choir. He left Malines at the age of 18 and moved to nearby Louvain, where he became choir conductor in the church of Saint Peter. In 1733 he was called to Bonn and became "Musicus" of the court. Bonn (Karl Mayer's print below shows a view of the city in Beethoven's times) was the capital of the Electors of Cologne. Courtly life was orderly, pleasant and congenial.*

Beethoven's grandfather was called to Bonn in the time of the Elector Clemens August, who liked pomp, women and music. Numerous festivities took place in the castle (above), and oratorios as well as Italian drama were performed. Casanova tells of a lively carnival with court ladies dressed in peasant costumes. However, Clemens August did not pay his subordinates well, and Beethoven's grandfather had to deal in wines in order to increase his earnings. Conditions improved under the Elector Max Friedrich. The birth date of Beethoven has not been ascertained. We do know that he was baptized in the church of Saint Remigius on December 17, 1770, and it is assumed that the child was born the day before. At right: The Birth of Beethoven *from a painting by Geselschap.*

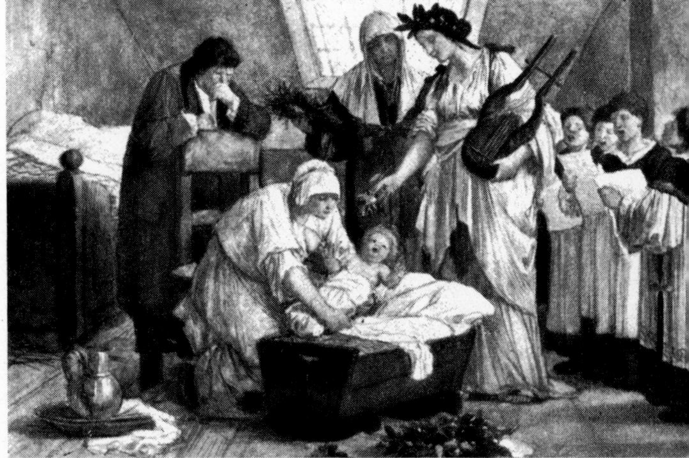

A GENTLE AND UNHAPPY MOTHER

Magdalena Kewerich, Ludwig's mother, from a painting at the Beethovenhaus. His love for her was deep and unfaltering.

Ludwig van Beethoven was born in Bonn on December 16, 1770. At the time his family lived on Bonngasse, in a modest home with a ceiling of decaying beams and a small garden overgrown with ivy and wild vines. Framed by a romantic landscape of hills, Bonn was then a small town of 8,000 inhabitants. A Romanesque cathedral overlooked the city, and the waters of the Rhine flowed past its ancient walls.

Beethoven's mother was Magdalena Kewerich, a woman of humble background. Daughter of a cook and widow of a waiter, herself a chambermaid, she gave birth to one of the greatest geniuses the world has ever known. She was an attractive woman of slight build, active, and of a sweet disposition. Her second husband, Johann, gave her eight children, the first of whom, Ludwig, died a few hours after birth. The second-born inherited the dead child's name. In ensuing years, Karl and Johann were born, followed in succession by three boys and a girl who died in infancy.

Ludwig grew up in an atmosphere of rustic simplicity. His childhood was not a happy one, but his gentle mother shielded her children from her husband's crudeness, and taught them respect for their eccentric and penniless father. From her, Ludwig learned patience in suffering and compassion for others.

Johann guessed that his son would achieve great stature as a musician. On May 26, 1778, Ludwig van Beethoven gave his first recital. Although he was seven years old, the invitations described him as being one year younger, as his father had set about the profitable task of turning him into a child prodigy.

In the fifteenth century the Bishop of Cologne and the electors, powerful princes of the Holy Roman Empire, had chosen Bonn as their episcopal seat. As a consequence, Bonn became an important cultural center that saw the growth of artistic endeavor and the rise of a university of the Enlightenment. Here the music of von Gluck, Mozart and Cimarosa, and the writings of Voltaire, Goldoni and Schiller were readily understood by a cultured and open-minded public.

Beethoven was born on the second floor of this building, in a small room badly lighted by a dormer window. The Beethovens lived there until 1774. They left because they could no longer afford the rent. In this old house and in the adjoining one, whose fronts face the Bonngasse, are collected the relics of Ludwig van Beethoven's life. On the left and above: three views of the house and an eighteenth-century print showing its front.

GENIUS MUST BE GENTLY GUIDED

With his disorderly hair and stocky build, Ludwig van Beethoven had a striking and rather coarse appearance. A dimple on the right side of his chin gave his face a curious asymmetry. His personality was a mixture of shyness and honesty, obstinacy and resolution, sadness and the desire to be loved. He had the friends and pastimes common to childhood. In the "gymnasium" he studied Italian and some Latin and French. He found mathematics difficult. Music, an "exact science" because it was based on measures, he understood well. By contrast, he could not complete a multiplication, and instead drew up the figures as many times as it was necessary, like an addition; but quavers and demiquavers held no secrets for him. He liked to play in the small garden of his house and in the parks of Bonn. But the long walks along the Rhine, his favorite pastime, were to remain his fondest memory of childhood.

Besides his father, a distant relation, Franz Rovantini, gave him piano and violin lessons. Excelling at the piano, Ludwig never completely mastered the violin. The organ, which he called "the sovereign of all instruments," inspired him with such awe that he never learned to play it well. His first noteworthy teacher was Christian Gottlob Neefe, who arrived in Bonn in 1779, and was appointed director of the National Theater. Neefe met the young Beethoven when he was barely 10 years old. He understood immediately the deep sensitivity of the boy. Above all, he realized that his genius must be gently guided and not stifled by rules and inflexible systems. Beethoven sensed that Neefe was a man far above the average and a loyal friend in whom he could confide. After a few years of association with the maestro, Beethoven could begin his first compositions: three sonatas, nine variations, a rondo and a piano concerto.

Neefe (above) was a distinguished musician, a man of letters, and an organist at the Court of Bonn. To him Beethoven owed the publication of his first works; among these was a piano concerto whose title page is reproduced here. Neefe was Beethoven's guide in music while the Breunings provided him with the restful atmosphere of an orderly and congenial family. He called their house (above, on the left) the "happy refuge." Beethoven, fascinated by the organ, learned to play it under the guidance of the Franciscan friar Willibald Koch. In the photograph below, on the left, the ancient organ of the Franciscans of Bonn on which Beethoven practiced as a boy. On the right: the stately cathedral of Bonn where he went often, following Neefe's advice, to listen to the solemn and imposing music of Bach.

The Elector Max Franz was the youngest child of the Empress Maria Theresa of Austria. An open-minded and intelligent man, he encouraged the arts and sciences, and abolished torture. In spite of these innovations, even his court was to be pervaded by the revolutionary spirit of contemporary France. The prince did not bestow favors by birthright, but according to individual merit. For this reason, among the young men of Bonn, he noticed and favored Beethoven, who, with his help, became, in May, 1789, a student of German literature at the University of Bonn. The Austrian nobleman Waldstein also furthered Beethoven's education by having him attend the performances of Shakespeare's dramas; through him, Beethoven acquired a good knowledge of the writers Kant, Lessing, Schiller and Goethe.

THE ELECTOR'S ORCHESTRA

Max Franz,
Elector of Cologne.

Ferdinand
von Waldstein.

The Archbishopric of Cologne was founded by Charlemagne; its archbishop was third Elector of the Holy Roman Empire and High Chancellor for Italian affairs. When the Elector Max Franz, Archbishop of Cologne since 1784, went with his court to the castle of Brühl (print below), he was accompanied by his entire orchestra. Concerts were given in the sumptuous baroque hall of the castle; Beethoven played the harpsichord and the viola in the orchestra. Fourteen years old at the time, he had been appointed second organist with the considerable yearly salary of 150 florins.

The Vienna Beethoven knew was already becoming the celebrated nineteenth-century capital with its wide avenues and imposing palaces. Three thousand carriages drove through the city at all hours of the day. Between six and eight o'clock in the evening, the Viennese liked to stroll along the shaded avenues. They lingered in the coffeehouses, where Germans, Slavs, Bohemians and Italians engaged in lively discussions. Bands played everywhere. In the restaurants, Italian oranges and Veronese salami were favorites. The best-dressed men wore blue frock coats and white trousers. For the ladies, small umbrellas in pastel colors were fashionable. In those times, Maria Theresa had the grounds of the Glacis, a sort of drill ground, leveled. Here, trees and flower beds were planted, and here also stretched out the beautiful avenues, always crowded with people. Below: a view of Vienna from the Belvedere, from a painting by Canaletto.

GLITTERING VIENNA

The artistic milieu of Bonn had become too confining for Beethoven. His friends loved and admired him; even the Elector Max Franz, enthusiastic patron of culture, held him in high esteem. But Ludwig looked beyond these tokens of admiration. He dreamed of going to Vienna, where he could meet the famous Mozart. When, in February, 1787, he obtained the elector's permission for the journey, he could hardly believe he was really leaving.

A rigorous winter had descended on Europe that year. Beethoven traveled by stagecoach, wrapped in furs, spending the nights in smoky wayside inns. Forgetting the journey's hardships, the 17-year-old Beethoven gazed at the mirage of a great city, which truly deserved its title of capital of music. In fact, in the last decades, Vienna had become a city of extraordinary allure. There all arts found fertile ground for their growth, but music, and particularly Italian music, held first place. The Emperor Joseph II had founded the Burgtheater. The Imperial Court had its own orchestra. In the patrician homes lived salaried artists. Even the wealthy bourgeois had their musical salons, and in the streets the barrel-organ played. The Austrian capital had thus become a symbol of contemporary culture in Central Europe. By the beginning of the nineteenth century it was the home of musical societies that supported opera and symphonic and chamber music.

On the left page: a German stagecoach of the early nineteenth century, on a road in Bavaria. In a similar coach, Beethoven traveled from Bonn to Vienna. Lasting almost a month, his trip took him through battle-ridden territories where the armies of the new French republic fought for the conquest of Europe. Above: a view of the Schönbrunn, one of the Hapsburg residences, from a painting by Canaletto. Left: a choral society of Vienna, the city where love for music was such that, people said, "even the little stone angels sang."

Among the musicians who taught music in Vienna at the end of the eighteenth century were Antonio Salieri, E. A. Förster, Johann Schenck and J. G. Albrechtsberger. They were also Beethoven's teachers. Salieri, in particular, instructed him in the difficult art of adapting music to song. Albrechtsberger gave him precious advice in the field of composing.

Antonio
Salieri

Emanuel Alois
Förster

Johann
Schenck

Johann Georg
Albrechtsberger

"WHY HAS THIS MAN COME TO TROUBLE US?"

By the end of the eighteenth century, Italian music predominated in Vienna. Enthusiastically receptive to all cultural currents in Europe, the Austrian capital had lost its artistic identity. Even Haydn, Handel and Mozart had traveled to Italy to perfect their techniques and bring back the fashionable "Italian style." However, through the perseverance of generous art patrons and the genius of its musicians, Vienna attempted to regain lost ground. With Beethoven, German music was to come into its own again. At the end of the eighteenth century, music was no longer the exclusive inheritance of powerful aristocrats, but spread to the lower social strata. A man of liberal ideas, Beethoven felt that music should reach all men, even the most humble.

Before Beethoven's rise to fame in Vienna, the public and the critics raved about the techniques of such pianists as Wölfl and Hummel. To prove his superior skill, Beethoven engaged in an open competition with the two musicians. He scored his first victory on March 29, 1795, playing his *Piano Concerto No. 2* at the Burgtheater. This was a music charged with meaning and depth hitherto unknown to the Viennese audiences. The public applauded enthusiastically but asked uneasily, "Why has this man come to trouble us?" Until then, even the great, like Haydn, wrote music for the ballroom. Now this "twenty-five-year-old lion" commanded attention by powerfully realizing philosophy in music. "He made one think." Well versed in music, the aristocracy understood the genius of the new composer and paved the way for his rise to fame.

At the end of the eighteenth century, Italian opera was the rage in Vienna. Amusing, effervescent and gay, it matched the personality of the Viennese. In the crowded theaters the works of Paisiello, Cimarosa, Paër and Cherubini were performed with great success. Beethoven himself attended the premiere of the Matrimonio Segreto *by Cimarosa. Drawing his inspiration directly from the themes of Italian opera, Beethoven wrote a series of variations. In the print on the left page: the city center of Vienna in Beethoven's time, and the house where he lived toward the 1800's, at No. 214 Graben. Above: the five-story house on the right belonged to the bookseller Trattener. In the background, on the left, was the shop of the editor Haslinger, a friend of Beethoven. The Maestro regularly patronized these shops.*

"THE WORLD SHALL SPEAK OF THIS YOUTH"

During Beethoven's first stay in Vienna, Mozart received him and even accorded him an audition. Worshiped by all of Europe as the musical genius of his times, Mozart was then 30 years old. At the audition, in spite of his excitement, Beethoven skillfully improvised a series of variations at the piano, but Mozart suspected him of having committed the music to memory. Beethoven asked for a second audition, proposing that the Maestro himself suggest a theme. Mozart consented. This time he was openly impressed by the young composer's genius. Deeply moved, he accepted him as his pupil, announcing to those present, "The world shall speak of this youth." Beethoven was to remember that Mozart himself never played in his presence.

In July, 1787, Beethoven's stay in Vienna was tragically interrupted. News had reached him that his mother was dying. He returned to Bonn immediately to be at her side. Shortly after, he wrote to his friend, Doctor von Schaden, "I found my mother in the worst of health; she had consumption. After enduring much pain and suffering, she finally died. She had been a good and loving mother, and my best friend." Deeply affected by his wife's death, Johann increased his drinking. Many a night Ludwig was compelled to do the round of Bonn's public houses in search of his father. In 1789 the old man was legally deprived of paternal authority. Ludwig was appointed head of the family, and thus became responsible for the support of his brothers.

Unlike Beethoven, Mozart liked to travel. On different occasions he had been to Paris, London, Holland, Rome and Prague. Active and friendly, he found himself at ease in any environment. When he met Beethoven in Vienna, he was writing his Don Giovanni. *Beethoven was only 17 years old, but he played without hesitation for the composer, celebrated by all the courts of Europe. Above: Beethoven improvises at the piano in Mozart's presence. Below: Beethoven, introduced by Mozart into Viennese society, plays the piano. On the left page: Mozart's house in Vienna, where he lived from 1784 to 1787. In the small print by Vigneron: Mozart's funeral. Neither friends nor relatives attended his funeral, and his body ended up in the common burial ground. Beethoven always carried with him a copy of this bleak scene.*

AN INVITATION FROM HAYDN

In July, 1792, the composer Franz Joseph Haydn, back from one of his frequent trips to London, was invited to Bonn by the Elector Max Franz. A luncheon and a concert were given in honor of the distinguished guest. On that occasion, Count Waldstein asked Haydn to listen to the *Cantata for Joseph II;* it had been written, he said, by a young man named Beethoven, a native of Bonn. Haydn accepted, and was genuinely impressed by the talented composer, to whom he made an unexpected proposal: "Not only do I encourage you to pursue further the study of music, but I also suggest that you continue it with me in Vienna."

Beethoven decided to accept Haydn's offer in spite of the personal problems he would have to overcome in order to leave. The financial responsibility for his family rested entirely on him, and he had to think of his own support in Vienna. In addition, he needed the consent of the elector. Waldstein himself took care of everything and even obtained two monetary grants for Beethoven. Knowing the young man's pride and his unwillingness to accept money as a gift, Waldstein told him that the grants were his by right as a repayment for his services at the court.

It was 1792 when Beethoven set out for Vienna. Mozart had been dead for a few months. Haydn was 60 years old, and the marvelous cycle of his compositions was not yet completed. The literary works of Rousseau were spreading throughout the Western world, and the Revolution was shaking the whole social structure of France. Beethoven, pervaded by the revolutionary spirit of the times, openly declared himself a republican. He was eager to study with Haydn, the inventor of modern symphony. But the old and placid maestro, involved with his own creative work, took little interest in his spirited pupil. Communion between the two artists proved impossible. Thus, after a year, Beethoven began to study secretly under the musician Johann Schenck. Georg Albrechtsberger and the Italian Antonio Salieri also instructed him, after Haydn's departure for London.

Returning to Vienna as Haydn's pupil, Beethoven went to live in an attic. He was careful to keep an accurate record of his expenses. Later he could rent better lodgings on the outskirts of the city, and play the piano as often as he wished. Below: Beethoven congratulates Haydn after the performance of his Creation *Mass. Left: Haydn rehearses for a concert in the castle of Esterhazy. At this time, Beethoven gained access to Viennese society. He ordered fashionable clothes and even took dancing lessons. In the princely homes of Vienna he appeared severe and dignified.*

Josef Gelinek, a Bohemian priest, was a great virtuoso who enjoyed the favor of the aristocracy. After having been "beaten" by Beethoven at a competition of piano improvisations, he described him thus: "He is not a man, but a devil. His improvisations are the most amazing thing I have ever heard." Right: Beethoven plays for his friends.

CONCERTS AND ACCLAIM

The conductor Gerhard H. Romberg and Cherubini have expressed the most reliable view on Beethoven the pianist. They declared that his manner of playing was harsh, hard, and amplified by excessive use of the pedal, but that his technique was daring, and his touch, especially in the "cantabili," of an almost sublime softness. Before playing, he used to run his finger along the whole length of the keyboard, like a mischievous child amusing himself. Left and below: Beethoven at the piano. Bottom: a drawing of his celebrated hands.

Until 1796 Beethoven was known in Vienna and in Germany as a virtuoso and not as a composer. Only later did his music come into prominence with the *Pathétique* in 1799, the *Spring Sonata* in 1800, and the *Eroica* in 1803.

After his concert of 1795 at the Burgtheater, his skill as a pianist opened to him an exciting career as a concert artist. He played in Prague, Berlin, Nuremberg and Dresden. His improvisations were particularly successful; one had to hear them, many reported, before one could fully appreciate his genius. "It is truly a pity that such divine inspiration should be lost," a Berlin critic once told him. Beethoven replied calmly that he could have played every note over again since nothing in his music was due to mere chance.

From time to time skilled pianists challenged him to play with them in public. Beethoven's performance always won the loudest acclaim. Hearing him play and losing courage, one of his rivals ran away from the concert hall and was never heard of again.

In June, 1796, Beethoven gave a series of concerts at the Royal Academy of Berlin. At the end of one of these performances, King Frederick William II presented him with a golden snuffbox filled with gold coins, a singular honor. These concerts also saw the reappearance of a distressing phenomenon. After the applause, an excruciating noise like a waterfall continued ringing in Beethoven's ears. He spoke to no one of these first signs of deafness, although he was already having trouble understanding everyday conversation.

Most of Beethoven's work was written after he became deaf. We must remember that in 1796 he was renowned only as a pianist. Thus his monumental work was created, in tragic anguish, by a composer who did not hear music.

PRINCES AND PATRONS

From the seventeenth century to the beginning of the nineteenth, artists lived and worked under the auspices of wealthy patrons. Literary awards, subsidies and copyrights did not exist. Instead, wealthy lords commissioned works of art and supported salaried poets, painters, and musicians. Like his contemporaries, Beethoven was subsidized by friends and admirers during his career as a composer. Thus we find compositions dedicated to such patrons as Waldstein, Rasoumowsky and the Archduke.

While still in Bonn, Ludwig had found in the friendly home of the Breunings a "happy refuge." In a congenial and peaceful atmosphere, guests and members of the family read from the classics or played music together. All were proud that Beethoven's renown as a pianist grew. Among them, Beethoven met young people of his own age, some of whom became his pupils. Also at the Breunings' he met the young Doctor Wegeler who was to marry Lorchen, Beethoven's first sweetheart, and remain his friend until death.

In 1792, another important personage entered Beethoven's life. He was Ferdinand Ernst Gabriel Waldstein, a generous patron of artists. A learned man, extremely influential at the Court of Bonn, he was also an amateur musician. "How can you play on such an old-fashioned piano?" he once said to Beethoven. "It is shameful!" A few days later four porters brought to the composer's house a new piano, the gift of Count Waldstein.

Two years after he had settled in Vienna, Beethoven became friendly with Count Moritz von Lichnowsky, one of the first among the notables of Vienna to recognize his genius. He offered Beethoven his hospitality, and placed at his disposal the quietest wing of his palace. At meals, Beethoven enjoyed the privilege of being the first served. But he was soon to abandon the palace for the modest lodgings on the Kreuzgasse; he began to eat at inns, the Ochs and the Schwann, both mediocre in quality. Yet here his creative vein seemed to find more congenial surroundings. Count Lichnowsky made him a yearly allowance and gave him two valuable violins, a Guarnerius and an Amati.

For many princes and nobles, it was a point of honor to support a musical group. The best concerts were held at the palaces of Lichnowsky and Kinsky, and of the Russian ambassador, Prince Rasoumowsky. The new music performed on these occasions was to become famous throughout the world. On the left page, above: Beethoven conducts the Rasoumowsky Quartet. *Below: the palace of Prince Kinsky. On this page, above: the Church of the Scotch. Below: the magnificent palace of Prince Rasoumowsky. Beethoven was held in high esteem by the nobility. If, in Mozart's times, the musicians were made to eat with the servants, Beethoven always occupied the place of honor at the table.*

Karl and Maria Christine Lichnowsky

Josephine and Johann Joseph Liechtenstein

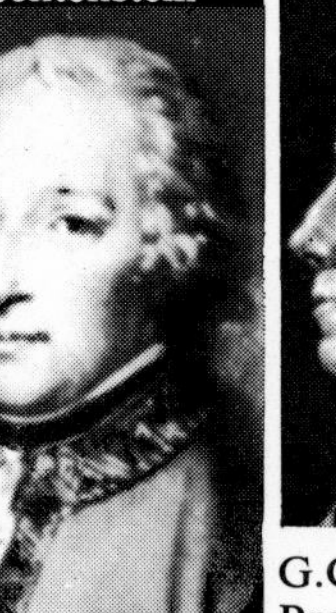

Gottfried von Swieten

Moritz Lichnowsky

G.G. von Browne-Camus

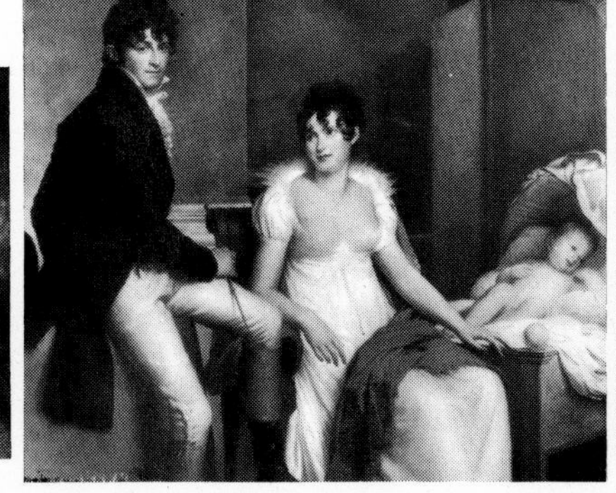

The von Fries Family

G.G. von Schwarzenberg

AN ARCHDUKE'S AFFECTION

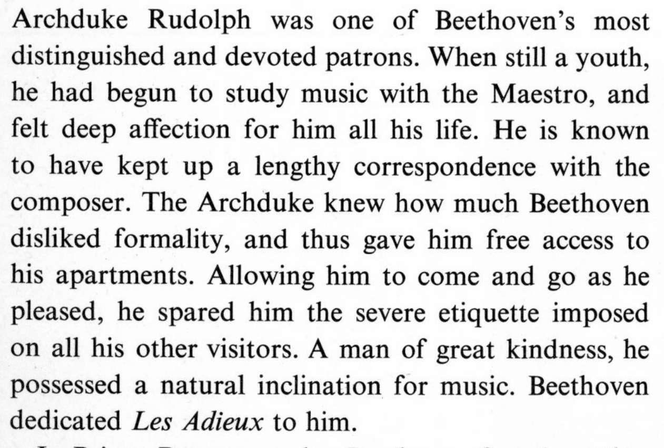

Archduke Rudolph was one of Beethoven's most distinguished and devoted patrons. When still a youth, he had begun to study music with the Maestro, and felt deep affection for him all his life. He is known to have kept up a lengthy correspondence with the composer. The Archduke knew how much Beethoven disliked formality, and thus gave him free access to his apartments. Allowing him to come and go as he pleased, he spared him the severe etiquette imposed on all his other visitors. A man of great kindness, he possessed a natural inclination for music. Beethoven dedicated *Les Adieux* to him.

In Prince Rasoumowsky, Beethoven found another distinguished patron for whom he composed a few magnificent quartets. The prince had a large collection of valuable paintings and an excellent library. In the sumptuous reception hall of his palace, Haydn and Beethoven attended the premieres of their own works.

A less devoted patron, but nevertheless a generous one, was Prince Lobkowitz, for whom music represented only a diversion. In 1804 the *Eroica* was performed privately at his palace.

Franz
Brentano

Archduke Rudolph, archbishop of Olmütz

Ferdinand
and
Caroline M.
Kinsky

F. Joseph
Lobkowitz

Franz
von Brunswick

Louis Ferdinand
of Prussia

A. Cyrillowitsch
Rasoumowsky

Nicholas
Esterhazy

J.M. von
Birkenstock

Ignatz von
Gleichenstein

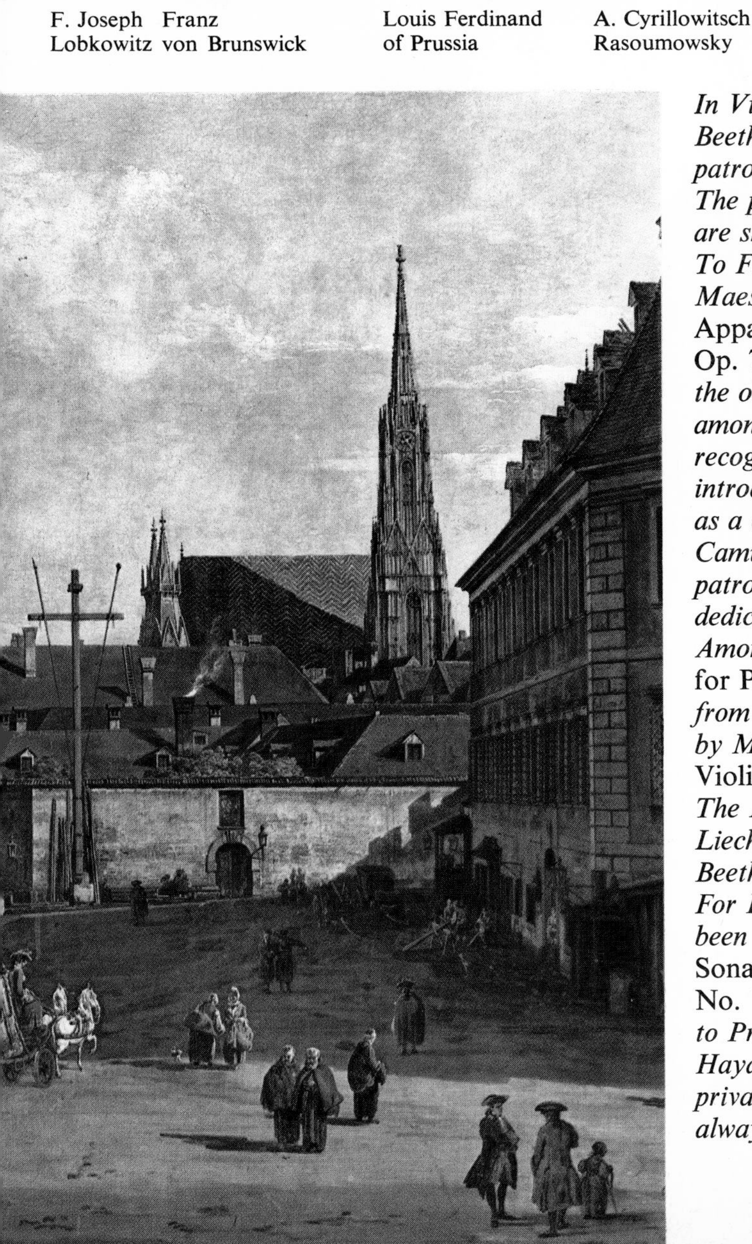

In Vienna and elsewhere Beethoven's friends and patrons were numerous. The portraits of a few of them are shown on these pages. To Franz von Brunswick the Maestro dedicated the Appassionata *and the* Fantasy, Op. 77. *Gottfried von Swieten, the organizer of a musical society among Viennese nobility, recognized Beethoven's talent and introduced him to his musical circles as a concertist. To Browne-Camus, whom he called "the first patron of my muse," the Maestro dedicated many compositions. Among them were seven* Variations for Pianoforte and Violoncello, *from a theme of* The Magic Flute *by Mozart, and three* Trios for Violin and Violoncello, Op. 9. *The Prince and Princess of Liechtenstein also belonged to Beethoven's circle of friends. For Princess Josephine, who had been his pupil, he wrote the* Sonata quasi una Fantasia, Op. 27, No. 1. *Beethoven was introduced to Prince Nicholas Esterhazy by Haydn, who was conductor at his private chapel. Young Ludwig was always well received by the prince.*

In spite of the subsidies that were seldom lacking, Beethoven was often without money. For this reason he decided once to leave Vienna. Judging the city frivolous and indifferent to his merits as a composer, he thought of accepting the appointment of Chapelmaster at Cassel. The new king of Westphalia, Jerome Bonaparte, had offered him a salary of 600 golden ducats to conduct an occasional concert, leaving him the rest of the time free for composing. As the news of his impending departure spread through Vienna, patrons and admirers met to find a way of preventing his leaving. To dissuade him from accepting Bonaparte's offer, a petition was circulated and signed in Vienna, while Archduke Rudolph, Prince Lobkowitz and Prince Kinsky committed themselves to making him a yearly allowance of 4,000 florins. In the end, Beethoven consented to remain. Left: the Lobkowitz palace where the premiere of the Eroica *was performed in private, from a painting by Canaletto.*

A POET'S MOTHER EAVESDROPS

Franz Grillparzer (1791–1872), rightly considered the greatest German poet, led a bitter and tormented life. His father died ruined financially by the Napoleonic wars. His mother committed suicide. He was employed by the government as a clerk. In poetry he tried to find an outlet for many hardships and humiliations. However, censorship and conservative critics opposed him in every way. Grillparzer was a poet of tragedy. In his works he dealt with the tragic themes then in vogue, but also opposed the sweeping wave of Romanticism in order to bring to light the real and often bitter emotions of man. One of his texts, Melusine, *was to be set to music by Beethoven. Kreutzer, instead, wrote the score. Right: the room where Grillparzer lived in Vienna.*

Beethoven used to say that too many of the emotions depicted in Romantic literature were unknown to him. By contrast, he felt close in experience and conception of life to the poet Grillparzer. Appropriately, it was Grillparzer who, in 1827, pronounced a moving oration at the composer's funeral in the cemetery of Währing.

When he met Beethoven for the first time at a musical soirée, Grillparzer was 15 years old. In his notes, he described the Maestro as rather lean, dark-complexioned, almost fastidiously dressed and wearing glasses to correct his short-sightedness. Two years later Grillparzer saw Beethoven again. He related thus his experience with the Maestro: "That year, I spent the summer with my parents at Heiligenstadt, a small town near Vienna. Beethoven had rented the rooms on the street side while we occupied the apartment facing the garden. We shared a common corridor that led to the stairway. My brothers and myself cared little for this strange man whom we heard muttering to himself whenever he passed us. Besides, he had become rather fat, and he went about dressed in a slovenly fashion. My mother, who had a great passion for music, loved to listen to him play at the piano. For this purpose she often went into the corridor. Standing near her door, but never approaching his, she would listen to him in ecstasy. However, one day, opening his door unexpectedly, Beethoven surprised her thus. He hurried back inside only to come out again shortly afterward, wearing his hat; he rushed down the stairs and out into the street. From that moment he stopped playing. In vain my mother assured him, through the servants, that no one would eavesdrop anymore, that our doors toward the garden would remain shut, and that even the other tenants would no longer use the main stairway, but the exit through the garden, even if that was the longer way around. Beethoven was adamant and did not play the piano until the fall, when we all went back to the city."

A ROMANTIC COMPOSER'S MANY LOVES

Love worked on Beethoven like a tonic. When he was in love, he became witty, polite, patient with those who made a nuisance of themselves, and even dressed with a certain refinement. He wanted to please, and knew how to please. In addition to being deaf, Beethoven was also short-sighted as a consequence of smallpox, and wore glasses since childhood. Yet, ugly, careless of his appearance, and so often stern, he appealed to women, who were attracted to him for his genius as a musician. Although unattractive himself, he always loved pretty women of high rank. Above: Beethoven plays for a group of ladies. Right: a painting illustrating the romantic climate at the beginning of the nineteenth century in Germany, The Cliffs of Rüge, *by F. C. David.*

Those who were close to Beethoven, as was Doctor Wegeler, affirmed that the great musician had been in love with different women all his life. Among the first women for whom he conceived a great passion was Giulietta Guicciardi, a young girl of Italian extraction. To her he dedicated the haunting *Moonlight Sonata.* But Giulietta, unheeding and selfish, was not worthy of the great man's love. In 1803 she married Count Gallemberg and went to live in Naples. Later, finding herself in financial difficulty, she asked Ludwig for help. He sent her money immediately. When she returned to Vienna years later, she tried to see her old admirer, but he refused to receive her. Yet he had suffered deeply for this woman, and even thought that for her sake he would abandon music forever.

In 1805 he fell in love with a young Hungarian, Marie-Thérèse von Brunswick. She came from an aristocratic family that had received him kindly when he had come to Vienna in 1799. He became friendly with her brother Franz and her sister Josephine. The two sisters became his pupils at the piano. In May, 1806, Ludwig and Marie-Thérèse became engaged. The deep love he felt for her was expressed in the *Fourth Symphony*, the *Sixth* ("Pastoral") and the *Appassionata.* However, in 1810, the dream of love was shattered. Reasons were perhaps his lack of financial means and the difference in social rank. In fact, the mother of Marie-Thérèse made it clear that she wished her daughter to marry someone of aristocratic birth. The two lovers did not see each other again, but Marie-Thérèse did not forget Ludwig and she refused to marry.

A year before his death, a friend found Beethoven with a portrait of Marie-Thérèse clasped to his heart. On the portrait she had written, "To the genius without equal, to the great artist, and to a worthy man."

WHO WAS THE IMMORTAL BELOVED?

The distinguished French novelist, André Maurois, has suggested that Beethoven had a daughter. According to this hypothesis, Beethoven fell in love with Josephine von Brunswick, and not with her sister Marie-Thérèse. Very different from her sister, Josephine was pretty, sweet-natured and rather shy. According to Maurois, she was the "Immortal Beloved." Widowed, she married the old Count Stackelberg. Although from May to December, 1812, Josephine and her husband did not see each other, a baby girl, named Minona, was born to her in April of the following year. Beethoven had in that period established a very close friendship with Josephine; he might have been the child's father. The most reliable historians, however, affirm that Marie-Thérèse, and not Josephine, was Beethoven's true love. Above: a walk in the outdoors. Right: some of the women Beethoven loved.

In May, 1810, during the intense period of his love for Marie-Thérèse, Beethoven met another woman, Bettina von Brentano. Beautiful and intelligent, she had lively dark eyes and the naïve appearance of a young girl. Very close to Beethoven, she sensed his suffering after the broken engagement with Thérèse and succeeded in relieving the sadness of that aftermath. To her friend Goethe she wrote: "Near Beethoven I have forgotten the world and you, O Goethe. . . . I do not think I am mistaken in believing him to be far ahead of our modern civilization."

There is no written proof of the relationship that existed between Bettina and Beethoven. Of the correspondence between the two, only one letter remains, too insignificant to be taken as evidence of a love relationship. It is known, though, that Bettina was admired by many great men, including Goethe, Louis of Bavaria, the brothers Grimm, and Franz Liszt. Bettina possessed true literary and musical talent. Hoffmann likened her voice to the sound of an organ with 30 registers.

Another fleeting love was the beautiful Thérèse Malfatti. Saucy, exuberant and gay, "the flighty Thérèse," as Beethoven called her, was not tormented by spiritual conflicts but gifted with a lively artistic temperament. She played the piano with great skill, and possessed a sensual contralto voice.

After Beethoven's death, three letters were found. Addressed to an unknown woman, without any indication of place or year, they carried the dates of the sixth and the seventh of July. These are letters of passionate love for an "Immortal Beloved" who shares fully the feelings of the composer, but who cannot marry him. Was she already married? Were the letters sent to the mystery woman and returned by her to Beethoven, or did he keep them without ever sending them to their destination? The romantic mystery remains unsolved.

Thérèse von Brunswick

Dorothea von Ertmann

Giulietta Guicciardi

Bettina von Brentano

Marianne G. von Westerholt

Eleanore von Breuning

Thérèse Malfatti

Rachel
Varnhagen von Ense

Marie von Erdödy

Josephine von Brunswick

Maria Leopoldina
Pachler Koschak

Amalie Sebald

Marie Bigot de Moroges

Elena von Breuning

THE THEATERS OF VIENNA

In Vienna, the capital of the Hapsburgs, even Emperor Franz delighted in playing the violin. This city, where music was played not only in the concert hall but also in homes, churches and the streets, had many theaters. One of these, the National Theater, had been commissioned by Joseph II. At the theater An der Wien, opera was performed, but even in the halls on the outskirts of the city, In der Rossau, Bein Fasan, and Auf der Wieden, musical performances were held. Concerts were given at the National Hof Theater, at the Zonzerthalle in Augarten, and at the Burgtheater. These theaters were patronized by an elegant public that lingered after the performances to discuss and comment at leisure.

In 1798 the noted French violinist, Rodolphe Kreutzer, came to Vienna with the retinue of General Bernadotte. He played in the presence of Beethoven, with whom he soon established a close friendship. Beethoven, enthusiastic about Kreutzer's technique, dedicated to him the Sonata in A for Pianoforte and Violin, Opus 47, *later called the "Kreutzer" Sonata. The violinist did not understand its greatness and, finding it "unintelligible," never thought of executing it. The first performer of the "Kreutzer" Sonata was the violinist Bridgetower, who played it in May, 1803, at the An der Wien. On the left page, above: the façade of the court theater and the Corinthian doors. Below: the Imperial Theater in Vienna's suburbs. This page, left: interior and façade of the Jägerstrasse Theater where the premieres of many works by Beethoven were held. Below: the National Hof Theater, in Saint Michael Square.*

SINGERS OF THE MAESTRO'S WORK

In the eighteenth century, singers were forced by the composers to engage in elaborate vocal gymnastics, reaching, at times, the point of convulsion while trying to hold certain notes. The choirs sang the most difficult vocal pieces and would often end their performance in a state of complete exhaustion.

Excellent singers were available to Beethoven. Anna Milder-Hauptmann, singer and actress of the school of Salieri, was the first interpreter of Leonora in the *Fidelio*. Gifted with a powerful voice that Haydn defined "as large as a house," she amazed the princes at the Congress of Vienna by the beauty of her voice in the cantata, *Der Glorreiche Augenblick*. ("The glorious moment"). The soprano Henriette Sontag was the first interpreter of the *Ninth Symphony* and of the *Missa Solemnis*. She was particularly successful onstage, where she could also demonstrate her talent as an actress. She retired from the theater when she married a diplomat in the service of the King of Sardinia. However, in 1848, as soon as her husband resigned from office, she made a triumphal return to the stage.

Fritz Demmer

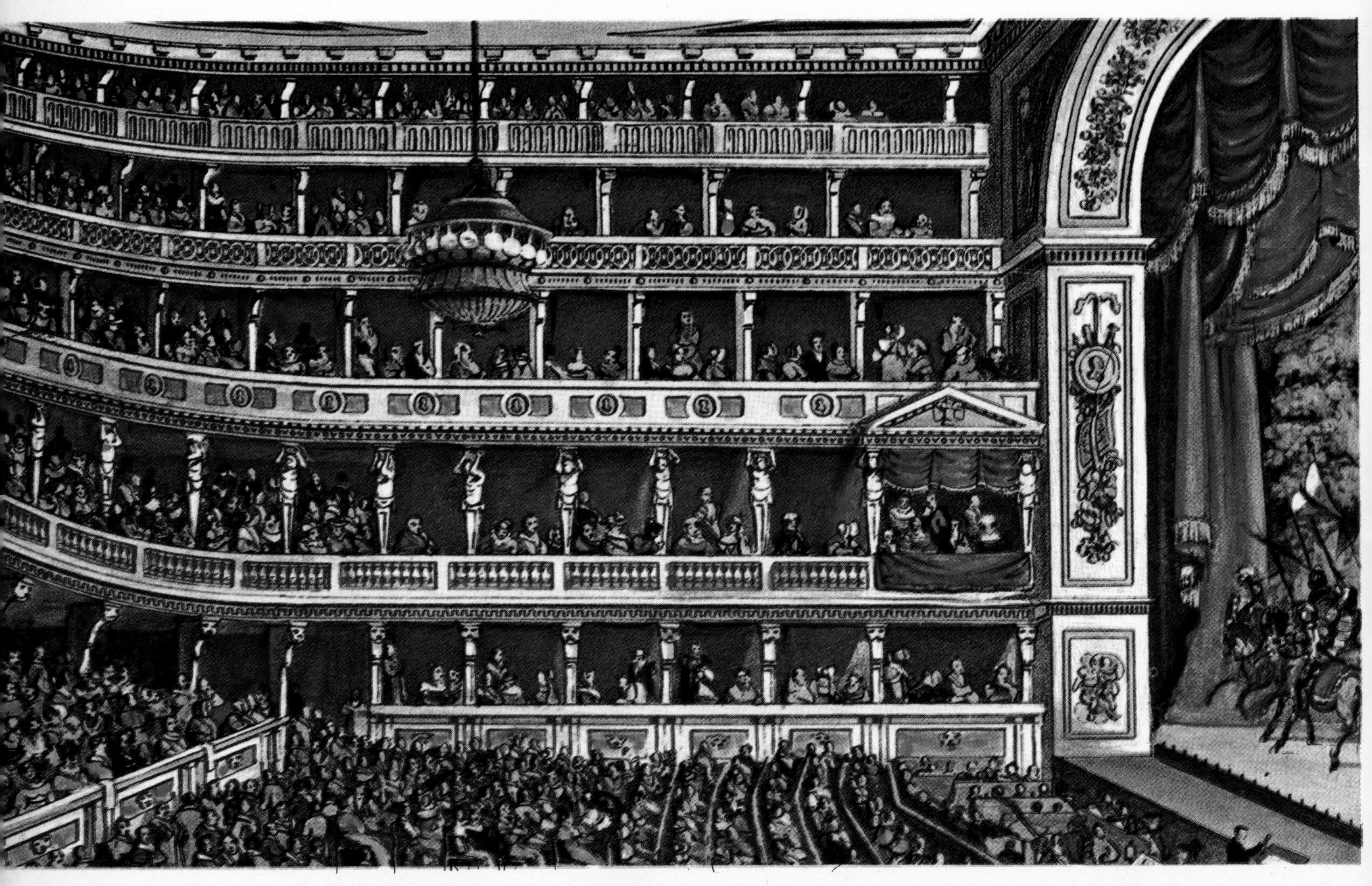

Anna
Milder-Hauptmann

Henriette Sontag

Franz Wild

Caroline
Unger-Sabatier

Anton Forti

The tenor Haizinger, the bass Seipelt and the contralto Caroline Unger-Sabatier were the first vocalists to sing in the Ninth Symphony *and in the* Missa Solemnis. *Caroline Unger-Sabatier often performed in Italy, where she was very popular. In 1843 she opened a school for singers in Florence. The tenor Fritz Demmer sang the role of Florestan in the first version of* Fidelio. *However, displeased with his performance, Beethoven blamed him for the opera's lack of success. At the repeat performance, the tenor August Roeckel and the soprano Wilhelmina Schroeder sang together. Beethoven wanted to write a new opera for the latter, but nothing came of it. She was friendly with the most distinguished musicians: Weber, Liszt, Schumann, Mendelssohn and Wagner. Nanette Schechner-Waagen, singer of the Vienna Opera House, once went to visit Beethoven confined in bed; she realized his fondest wish by singing the aria of Leonora in* Fidelio. *"You gave a masterful performance," said the composer, moved, when she had finished. "I thank you for the fine lesson." The choreography of the ballet,* The Men of Prometheus, *whose music was composed by Beethoven in 1800, was the work of Maria Casentini, prima ballerina at the Burgtheater.*

Anton Haizinger

Nanette
Schechner-Waagen

Maria Casentini

THE NEED FOR PUBLISHERS

The publishers found in Beethoven a prolific composer whose work was much in demand and earned them good returns. His catalogued compositions number 138, without taking into account his early works. His entire work consists of 9 symphonies, 32 piano sonatas, 10 sonatas for violin and piano, 5 concertos for piano and orchestra, 15 quartets, the Fidelio, *the* Missa Solemnis, *the* Septet, *in addition to trios, quintets, serenades and bagatelles. On the right: Vienna's Kohlmarket, where the Artaria Publishing House had its office. Above: the publishers Steiner, Artaria, and Haslinger. Below: Haslinger's music shop.*

In the eighteenth and nineteenth centuries, a composer's success was dependent on the farsightedness of his publishers. In fact, a composition could not be presented to the public without having first been bought by a publisher. He paid a certain sum of money to the musician, commensurate with the importance of his composition. Subsequently he printed the score and distributed it to the orchestras of Europe.

In a moment of discouragement, Beethoven said of his publishers, "They feed on my lifeblood and, to me, they give nothing." Among those who bought his music were Christoph G. Breitkopf and Gottfried C. Härtel. Their publishing house, the foremost in Europe, had its main office in Leipzig, and also printed works by Haydn, Mozart, Chopin, Liszt, Schubert, Schumann, Brahms and Wagner. In addition, many of Beethoven's compositions were published by the cousins Carlo and Francesco Artaria, who were also devoted friends. Their main office was in Vienna. They compiled a valuable collection of 93 manuscripts of works by Beethoven. When they ceased publication in 1932, all of the valuable material they had gathered went to the National Library of Berlin.

Clementi and Pleyel became publishers for the express purpose of helping Beethoven to bring his music to the audiences. To them he sold, for 200 pounds, his "Rasoumowsky" quartets, the *Fourth Symphony*, the *Coriolan* overture, and the *Concerto for Violin and Orchestra*. We must also remember the publishers Nicholas and Peter Simrock, father and son, with their main office in Berlin, in addition to a number of others: Hoffmeister and Kühn, Haslinger, Scheissinger, and Thomson, the latter from Edinburgh. To him we owe the collection of Scottish Songs, also by Beethoven. All of these publishers often urged Beethoven to give them new compositions to bring before the public; it had become fashionable among them to print his music, but they were also convinced of his genius.

The dedication of music to wealthy and powerful personages was a source of income for nineteenth-century composers. However, Beethoven dedicated his works almost exclusively to friends and acquaintances, accepting in exchange only an occasional gift. At times, with the dedication of a composition, he returned favors or remedied an offense brought about by his explosive temper.

KUNSTHANDLUNG . ARTARI

THE PORTRAITS

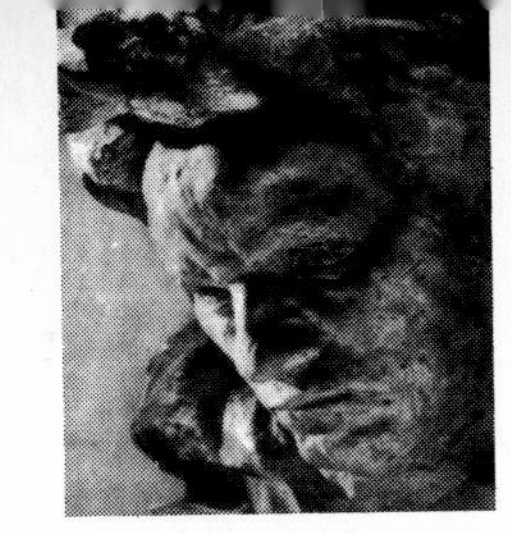

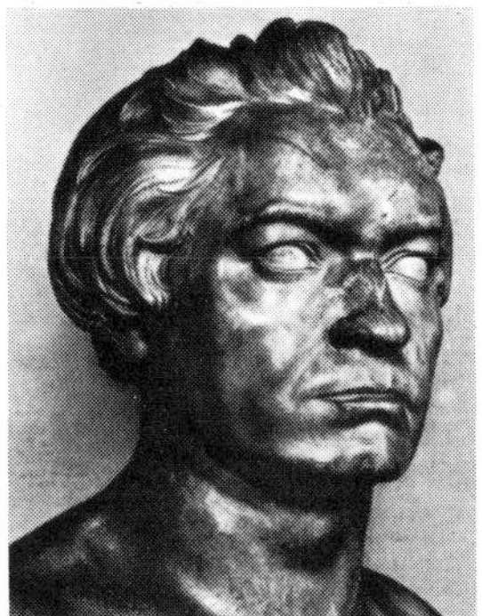

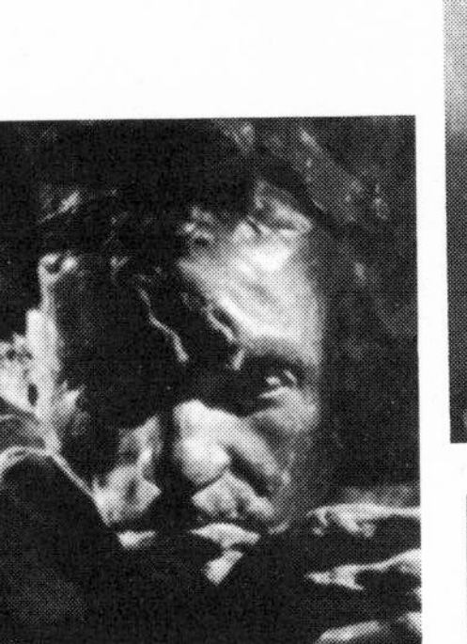

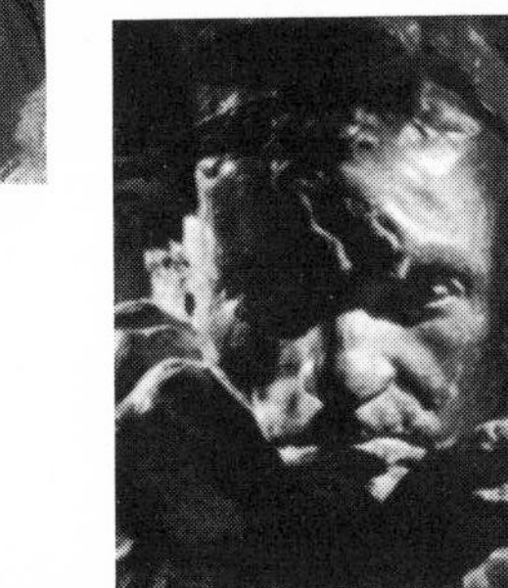

A penetrating gaze and strong features characterized Beethoven's face. Stern and grave like a dramatic mask, reflecting all of his internal moods, his face intrigued painters because it lent itself to a wide variety of artistic interpretations. Center, in full color: a nineteenth-century portrait of Beethoven by an unknown artist.

THE TRAGIC APPROACH OF DEAFNESS

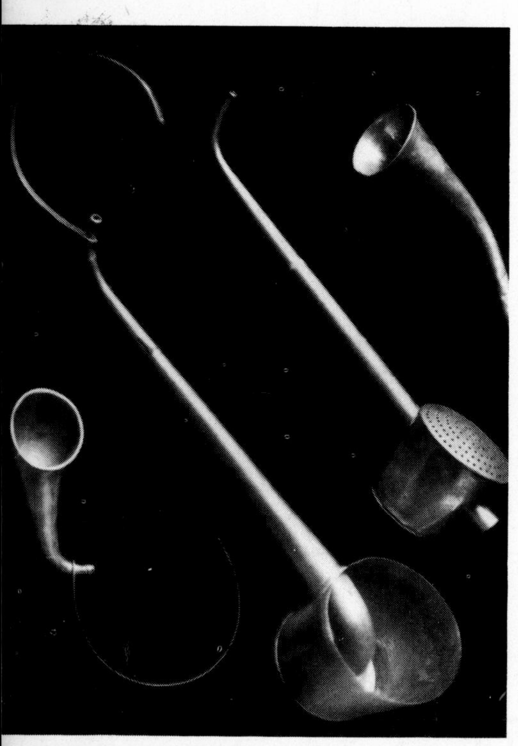

What caused Beethoven's deafness? Some called it the consequence of his father's heavy drinking, or even of his mother's illness, tuberculosis of the lungs. Others believed it was caused by too frequent ice-cold showers. Modern medicine can give us a reliable answer. His deafness was due to otosclerosis, the growth of a spongy bone inside the ear. Today, an operation or a hearing aid can easily remedy this fault. However, the large hearing aids at the beginning of the nineteenth century drew ridicule on those who had to use them, besides failing to help the hearing to a significant degree.

Increasing concern about his deafness troubled Beethoven between 1796 and 1800. Although he was gradually losing his hearing and an annoying whistling noise echoed constantly in his ears, Beethoven told no one about his difficulty.

In the spring of 1801 Beethoven played at the house of friends. The elegant men and ladies gathered around him realized suddenly that, in the pianissimi, Beethoven's hands hardly touched the keyboard. Wondering, they did not realize that he was already deaf. The Maestro imagined that the keys released delicate notes; instead, his fingers moved lightly in silence. That evening someone began to suspect that Beethoven was ill, and that perhaps some infirmity was depriving him of the use of his hands.

On June 1, 1801, Ludwig finally confided to his friend Karl Amenda the mental agony imposed on him by deafness: "Your Beethoven is terribly unhappy. Know that the noblest part of my being, the hearing, has now weakened. . . . My illness grows worse; I do not know whether I shall ever recover. . . ." In the same month he wrote to Wegeler, "It is almost two years since I have given up the company of other people because I cannot say to them, I am deaf! Such a confession would be easy if I practiced another profession but, for a musician, such a predicament is horrible." When he went to the theater, he began to sit close to the orchestra in order to hear the singers. Sometimes he grasped sounds, but not words. He could not bear that anyone should raise his voice so that he could hear.

Beethoven never became totally deaf. Even at an advanced age, he could distinguish the low tones. Yet, for a musician, who needed to hear everything in a composition down to the last nuance, this was of little comfort. In 1802 his physician, Doctor Schmidt, sent him to spend the summer at Heiligenstadt, a peaceful retreat where he could rest his ears. It was a summer of despair. No one knew of it until, after Beethoven's death, the will addressed to his brothers was disclosed.

Deafness compelled Beethoven to stop playing the piano. He gave himself up completely to composition, thus giving the world some of the greatest music ever written.

Heiglnstadt
am 6ten October
1802

"FELLOW MEN, YOU DO ME A GREAT WRONG!"

In 1802, having completed the *Second Symphony* and about to begin the *Third*, Beethoven faced a deep crisis. He had just dedicated the *Moonlight Sonata* to Giulietta Guicciardi when she left him. On October 6, 1802, Beethoven wrote in despair a letter to his brothers with the instructions: "To be read and carried out after my death." The letter has become known as the "Testament of Heiligenstadt." It is believed that a few days before writing it, Beethoven had contemplated suicide. The Testament opens with the following words imbued with sadness: "Fellow men, who believe or say that I am ill-tempered and your enemy, you do me a great wrong! You do not know the secret reason for what is mere appearance. My heart and my thoughts, since youth, were impelled by all that was good. I was prepared to accomplish great deeds. But think, for six years I have been afflicted by an incurable illness. . . . How I was mercilessly thwarted by the repeated and sorrowful experience of my bad hearing! Yet I could not say to men, speak louder, shout, for I am deaf! How could I confess to the weakness of a sense that in myself ought to have been more perfect than in others?"

Yet, if the predominant tone of the letter is despair, the Maestro also shows that, in his art, he has found renewed strength, thus overcoming the temptation of suicide: "What humiliation if someone near me heard a distant flute, and I heard nothing. If someone heard a shepherd sing, and I still heard nothing. These events led me to despair! I almost took my own life! Only music could hold me back. I felt it impossible to leave this world before having fulfilled my calling. Only thus did I preserve this wretched life."

After naming his two brothers beneficiaries of the will, and having thanked Prince Lichnowsky, Beethoven concluded the Testament with a poignant appeal: "Divine Providence, show me at least a single day of pure joy. For too long a time true happiness has eluded me! When, O God, shall I feel it once more?"

Heiligenstadt was a residential area a few kilometers from Vienna. Beethoven lived there in 1802, following Doctor Schmidt's advice to rest his hearing in the peace and solitude of the country. However, Beethoven faced, during his isolation in Heiligenstadt, a tragic crisis whose signs are reflected in the music of the Eroica. *He was 31 years old at the time, and his best compositions remained to be written. He appeared to live only for music. Walking in the street, he would stop abruptly. Taking a notebook from his pocket, he would jot down a sudden inspiration. This would later be the object of long study and meditation in the quiet of his rooms. On the left page: part of the text from the Testament of Heiligenstadt and, below, the house where Beethoven wrote his dramatic confession. On this page: the church of Heiligenstadt in Beethoven's times, from a print by L. Janscha.*

DAILY LIFE OF A GENIUS

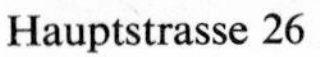
Hauptstrasse 26

Grinzingerstrasse 64

Pfarrplatz 2

Auerspergstrasse 3

Billrothstrasse 62

Hadikgasse 62

Beethoven's day began early in the morning. As soon as he was up, he went to his desk to make a note of some idea that had come to him during the night. He might also review a composition finished the previous evening. Then he proceeded to wash and dress. It has often been reported that Beethoven was careless about his person. Although he was not a dandy, he certainly liked physical cleanliness. It is probable that during periods of intense creativity he did not shave, or that he washed hurriedly or, again, that he did not change the collar of his shirt. Nevertheless, he usually took a shower in the morning, throwing on himself so much ice-cold water that it flooded the floor, causing the servants and the tenants below to complain. After the shower he made coffee. There had to be sixty grains, which he counted one by one. Then he sat at his desk or at the piano to work. Later in the morning he would take a long walk. In the street he would stop to look at the shop windows. Most of all he was fascinated by the displays of secondhand dealers. In fact, his house was filled with objects of all kinds. Some were beautiful and of great value, but others were merely odd. Although he appreciated good food, he ate irregularly. The afternoon hours were spent working, but he often went for a long walk in the country. Dinner, taken at no fixed time, was light. Sometimes it consisted only of soup. In the evening he paused to read a few pages by writers such as Goethe, Schiller, Homer, Plato and Shakespeare. Then he retired for the night, and in slumber he finally found rest.

Kärntnerstrasse 33

Mölkerbastei

Ballgasse 6

Ungargasse 5

Hetrendorferstrasse 75

Kahlenbergerstrasse 26

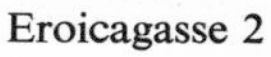

Eroicagasse 2

Probusgasse 6

Tiefergraben

Theater of Vienna

In Beethoven's house, servants came and went as in few others. The composer was intolerant of even the most insignificant incidents. A small theft by a maid or a negligent laundress would cause endless tragedies. Among the numerous servants who succeeded each other in his service, a few understood that they were dealing with a man above the average, and patiently bore his frequent outbursts of temper. The housekeeper, Mrs. Schnapps, established a certain measure of order and peace, taking an active interest in "the dear gentleman," as she liked to call him. In spite of her attentions, Beethoven spared her neither reproaches nor threats, nor even the throwing of eggs, if he suspected that they were not fresh. In short, Beethoven changed servants almost as often as he changed lodgings. During his 35 years in Vienna, he moved 30 times, always in search of peaceful surroundings, more fresh air and more light. On these two pages: some of the houses he occupied in Vienna.

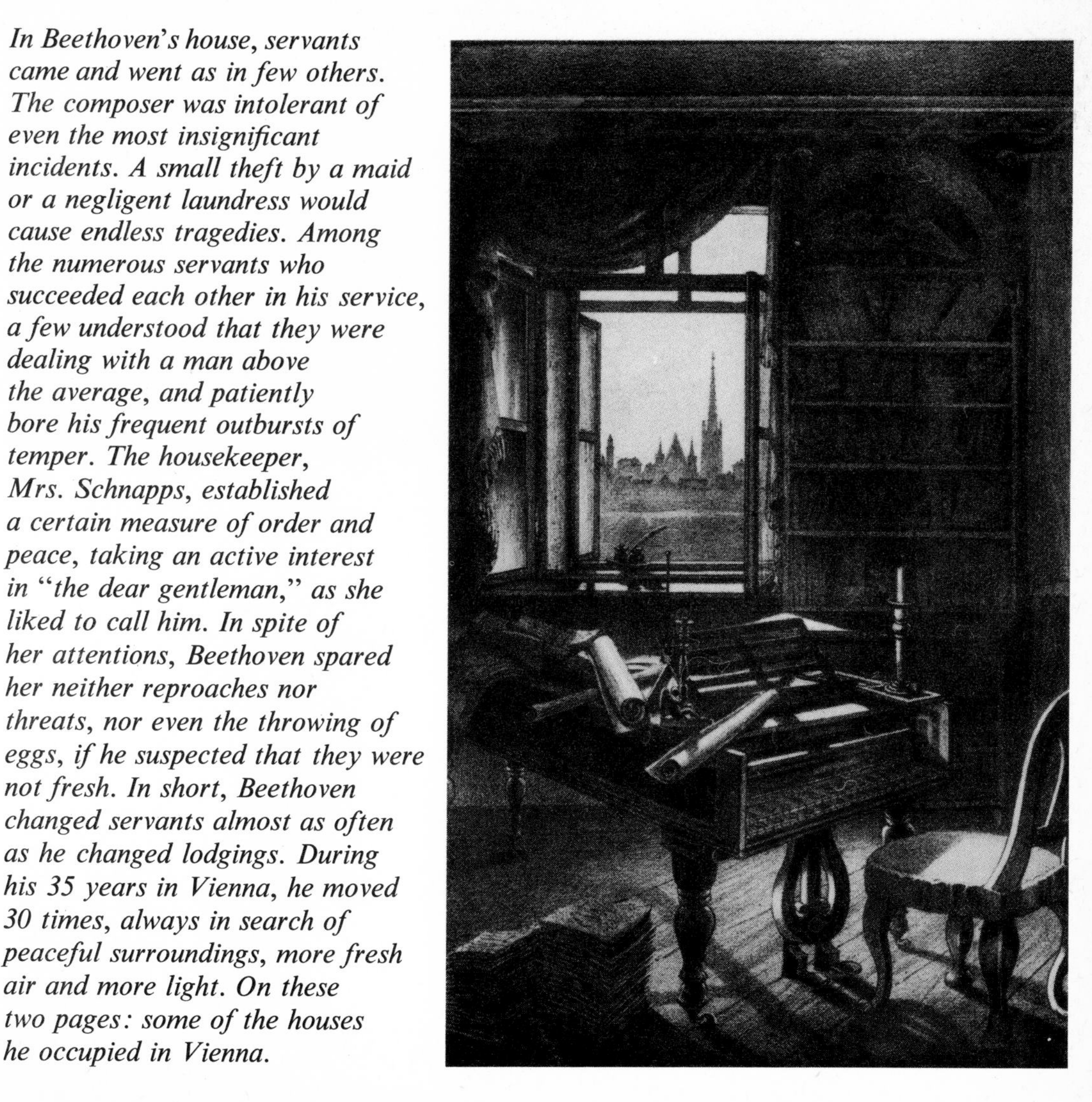

QUICK TO ANGER, QUICK TO REPENT

August von Klöber, who spent much time with Beethoven while painting his portrait, described him thus: "I saw him stop often, pencil stub in hand, as if listening intently, and then write something in a notebook. His hair was steel-colored. When he spoke, particularly with people he liked, he assumed a benevolent and mild expression. Every internal mood was instantly reflected on his countenance." Below: Beethoven strolling in a park, from a nineteenth-century print. On the right page: caricatures depicting the Maestro in some typical attitudes.

What was Beethoven really like? The opinions of his contemporaries are as varied and contradictory as his moods. Some described him as being laconic, sullen and unsociable, bad-tempered, and careless of his appearance. Others believed him communicative, genial and sociable, neat and even-tempered. In reality an impetuous man, he took offense easily but would promptly regret it.

The pianist von Bernard, who knew him well, wrote, "He was short and ugly. His face was covered with smallpox scars. His hair was intensely black, and he dressed without the customary refinement of our social circles. He spoke with the accent of the Rhineland and used unpolished expressions. Often he was rude. Once I saw the eccentric Countess Thun kneel at his feet and beg him to play. . . ."

Everyone seemed to agree that he was generous, ready to help others, and unusually kindhearted. Despite his coarse appearance, Beethoven was a man of high moral qualities, thirsty for knowledge, and entirely committed to the difficult task of spiritual purification. An episode that took place at Troppau, near Graz, shows how proud and sensitive a man he was. He had been invited to the castle of Prince Lichnowsky to play for a large gathering of French officers. Preparing to play, he noticed that a few among his audience had not interrupted their conversation to listen. At that, Beethoven turned abruptly and left the room. In religion he was a freethinker but believed in a Supreme Being, a measure of all perfection. His mind, like his art, was in continual and dramatic evolution. As a composer, he did not intend to be an innovator, although his music was definitely "avant-garde." He used to say, "When new ideas come to me, I do not realize it, but I hear others identify them."

His innovations were misunderstood by the conservatives, and often remained unintelligible to those still bound to the school of Mozart and Haydn. However, in Vienna, a few were already saying, "This man will console us for the loss of our Mozart."

Beethoven liked to eat out with his friends. During the hours spent in good company at the table, he relaxed and let himself go. Often he surprised his companions by his humor. At times his noisy mirth dismayed his friends, so used to his stern countenance. Right: the Silver Café on Spiegelgasse, from a lithograph by Katzler. In a few inns, musicians met to present their compositions. At Zum wilden Mann, Beethoven had his quartets performed by the famous Schuppanzigh group. Associating with a lively and gay circle of friends, Ludwig learned to drink champagne. However, he made a serious effort to abstain from drinking because, as he wrote to his friend Kuhlau, "these things stifle me rather than stimulate my creative vein." Moreover, the memory of his alcoholic father was a warning to him. In the prints below and on the right page: the coffeehouse in the park on Vienna's ramparts; the exterior of the concert hall at the Augarten; the Inn of the White Swan at the new market.

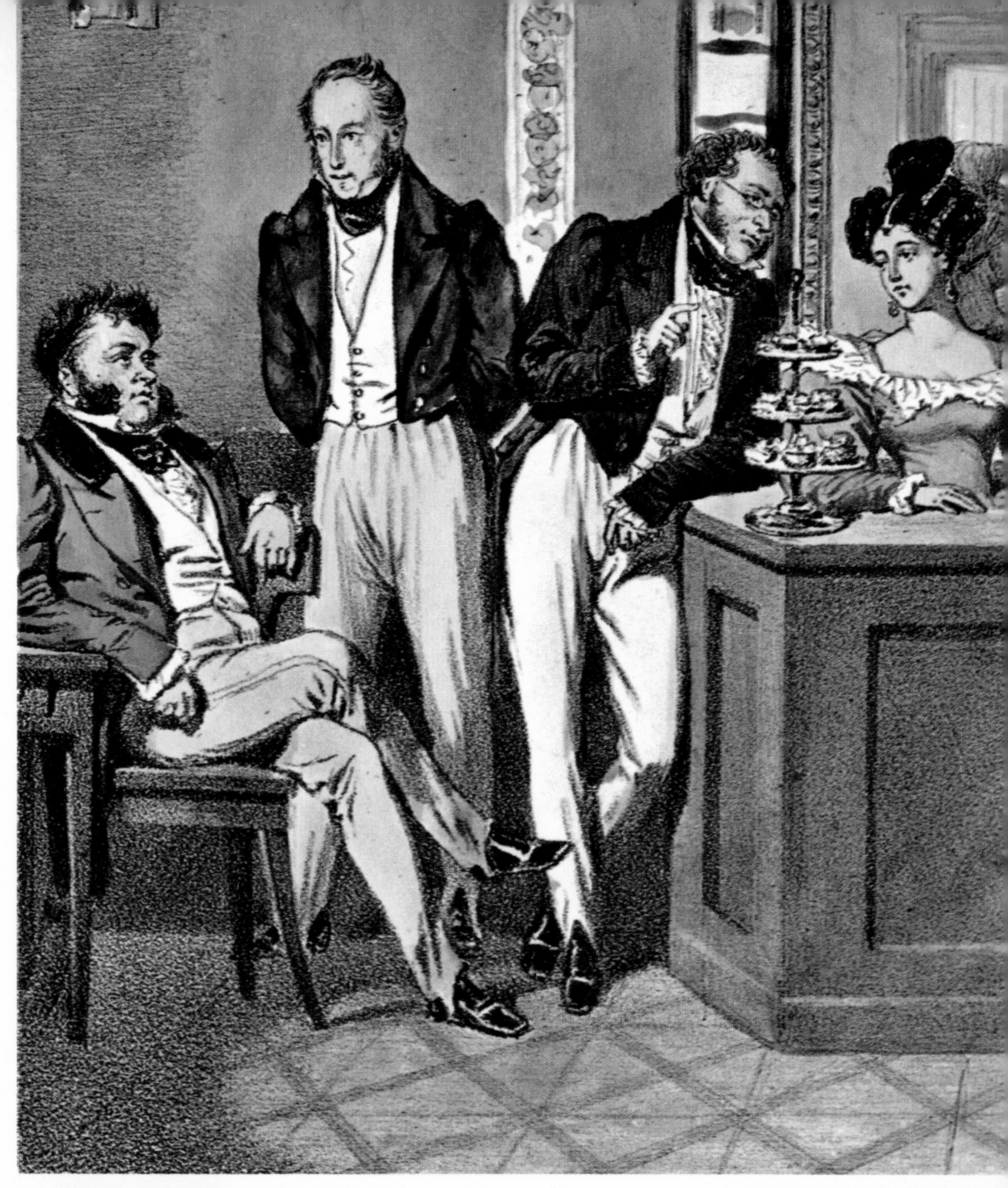

THE COFFEEHOUSES OF VIENNA

Ludwig van Beethoven went out every day because he enjoyed walking. If the sky was clear, he went to the country. If it rained, he remained in the city. Walking slowly through the streets of Vienna, he lingered in front of the shops. Often he went into the coffeehouses and pubs. Like all Viennese, Beethoven liked to walk in the Prater, the large park at the city gates. Owned in the past by the imperial family, this park had been opened to the public by the Emperor Joseph II. It had magnificent, broad avenues where carriages came and went. Here and there, where the trees formed natural amphitheaters, orchestras played, alternating operatic and symphonic music with military marches. Under the tall chestnut trees were open cafés patronized by a congenial and lively crowd. Notebook in hand, the Maestro wandered among the crowds of strollers, lost in reverie. Children ran up to him and offered him flowers.

Frequently, on leaving the Prater, he went to meet his friends at the Hotel of the White Swan, at the Black Camel, or at the City of Trieste. In these fashionable coffeehouses, in the midst of tobacco smoke and the pungent smell of alcohol, varied themes related to art and thought kindled discussion. Beethoven entered and seated himself at a table. He ordered a glass of beer and, closing his eyes, smoked a large pipe. If a friend touched him on the shoulder, he opened his eyes suddenly, as if waking from a dream. He took out his "conversation book" and demanded loudly that his interlocutor write down his question. Well informed on current events, he liked to talk politics. And at the popular music shops, he could meet the people of his own world—publishers, composers and music lovers.

FRIENDS AND PUPILS

Among Beethoven's closest friends was Karl Ferdinand Amenda, a violin teacher at the school of Mozart's widow. He was an unassuming man, learned in theology, short of money, but endowed with goodness and talent. The two met in 1796, during a musical soirée at the house of mutual friends. That evening Amenda played the violin for a string quartet. Beethoven invited him to his house for the following day. Music and talk filled the afternoon. When Amenda took his leave, Beethoven accompanied him home. There they spoke and played some more. When it was time for Beethoven to go, Amenda walked him home in his turn, and so on, back and forth until dawn. A close friendship was born between the two men, of a kind Beethoven had shared only with Doctor Wegeler and the Breunings.

The Maestro also made friends among his pupils. Closest to him were Ferdinand Ries and Karl Czerny. However, only Ries was formally acknowledged by Beethoven as his pupil. Czerny became one of the most distinguished virtuosos of his times. He wrote hundreds of exercises and compositions, still fundamental today to the study of piano. Czerny relates that frequently, at the end of a long improvisation, Beethoven discouraged the admiration of those who were present with a harsh laugh and exclaimed, "But you are all mad!" He never took his improvisations seriously, even when he wrote them down. Ries adds that he used to pile the manuscripts in a corner of the room, in the midst of indescribable disorder.

Ignatius Schuppanzigh was also an intimate friend of Beethoven. A violinist, he took care of the distribution of Beethoven's music for string quartets. The Maestro called him Falstaff because of his large frame. Count Zmeskall, nicknamed "Count Music," was a friend to whom Beethoven often turned for help. Another friend was Nanette Streicher. Wife of the famous piano manufacturer, she would patiently run Beethoven's chaotic household, where books of music mingled on the floor with dirty dishes, half-emptied bottles, jackets and slacks. Beethoven's last years were enlivened by a merry fellow, Karl Holz, with whom the Maestro amused himself in making up word games.

Franz Gerhard Wegeler

Muzio Clementi

Karl Ferdinand Amenda

Anton Reicha

Karl A. von Malchus

Anton Diabelli

Ignatius Schuppanzigh

Anton Schindler

Nanette Streicher

Ferdinand Ries

Karl Czerny

Rodolphe Kreutzer

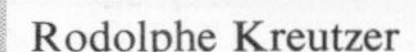

Karl Holz

S. von Breuning

A close friend of Beethoven during his last years was Anton Schindler, a young student who became his secretary. Beethoven held him in high esteem. However, he did not spare him reproaches and anger. In spite of his difficult personality, the friendships Beethoven established did not dissolve easily. Some lasted a lifetime. The friends who succeeded in understanding his complex personality and had an intuition of his genius kept their affection for him in spite of his whimsies and outbursts. They soon discovered that he was generous and kind. Below: Saint Michael Square in Vienna. On the left page: a few of Beethoven's friends from Bonn and Vienna.

WAR COMES TO VIENNA

Four years after the Battle of Austerlitz, Napoleon's armies repelled the assault of the Austrian troops and, in a difficult reconquest, tightened their hold around Vienna. On May 13 the French bombarded the suburbs of the Austrian capital. While cannon boomed close to the city walls, the court and the nobles fled. Beethoven took cover in the basement because each roar of the cannon resounded painfully in his eardrums. The pain was so sharp that he had to hold two pillows pressed against his ears. During the siege, all concerts were suspended; musicians soon found themselves in economic distress. Beethoven tried to help his friends by collecting money from publishers and from the few nobles still in the city. The danger of inflation drew near. Beethoven lost his allowance of 4,000 florins, offered by Archduke Rudolph to keep him in Vienna. Meanwhile, the old Haydn died after long illness. Beethoven mourned this loss and, badly dressed, ill and in pain, followed the coffin of the "venerated Maestro" over the roads leading to the cemetery, while the French army watched.

"FIDELIO"— A NEAR FAILURE

The Fidelio, *Beethoven's only opera, has no stylistic or structural innovations to distinguish it from Italian opera. Above and on the opposite page we see sketches for a few scenes of the* Fidelio, *and the program for its premiere. Another musical composition for the stage is the* Egmont *overture, a drama by Goethe whose pronounced ideas on freedom had captured the Maestro's imagination. In the* Fidelio *heroism, faithfulness and conjugal love are celebrated. Beethoven's best compositions do not adhere to fixed themes, dogmatic moral precepts or concrete subjects. All these were limitations to his creative genius. He liked to delve deep into the human heart and to roam freely in the unbounded spaces of the spirit.*

Neue Oper.

Heute Mittwoch den 20. November 1805
Wird in dem k. auch k. k. priv. Schauspielhaus an der Wien
gegeben:
Zum Erstenmal:

Fidelio,
oder:
Die eheliche Liebe.

Eine Oper in 3 Akten, frey nach dem Französischen bearbeitet
von Joseph Sonnleitner.
Die Musik ist von Ludwig van Beethoven.

Personen.

Die Handlung geht in einem Spanischen Staatsgefängnisse, einige Meilen von Sevilla vor.

Die Bücher sind an der Kassa für 15 kr. zu haben.

Preise der Plätze:

Die Logen und gesperrten Sitze sind bey dem Kassier des k. auch k. k. National-Theaters zu haben

Der Anfang um halb 7 Uhr.

It is tragic and disheartening to think that Beethoven suffered through years of poverty, although his contemporaries acknowledged his genius. His patrons dead or vanished, he owned only one pair of wornout boots. Once he even had to borrow a mirror from his admirer "Count Music."

The inventor of the metronome, Mälzel, who also made Beethoven's ear trumpets, suggested that he compose a symphony in honor of General Wellington's victory over Napoleon's armies. Beethoven, harassed by debts, agreed, and in a short time composed *Wellington's Victory*. All of Vienna's famous musicians were at the premiere, among them Spohr and Meyerbeer. After a success that greatly enhanced his popularity, Beethoven was urged by his friends to write an opera. Although, as a musician, he did not have a marked inclination for the theater, he set to work to rewrite his *Fidelio*.

Finished in May, 1814, the *Fidelio* scored a triumphal success. Beethoven himself conducted the premiere, but the musicians in the orchestra and the singers looked only at the substitute conductor, Umlauf. Behind the deaf Beethoven, he directed the entire performance, which would otherwise have ended in utter disaster. The *Fidelio* captivated the audiences of Prague, Leipzig and Berlin. Pleased with its success, Beethoven returned to Vienna in September of the same year.

In the Austrian capital, all the princes of Europe were about to convene after the defeat of Napoleon's armies. Weissbach, a Salzburg lawyer, wrote about the Maestro at about that time: "In spite of the sturdiness of his body, he is ill. Nature has kept him tied to the world by few and delicate strings. His musical sense is such that he can do without his hearing. In all my life, never have I met a heart more simple, or a more inflexible will."

In those years, while composing, Beethoven had to hold between his teeth an acoustical stick of wood. By pressing it against the piano, he could grasp some of the musical vibrations released while he played.

Beethoven's fame is due almost entirely to his symphonic compositions (symphonies, quartets, sonatas, concertos), moving to audiences because of their deeply felt spirituality. The great orchestra conductors have always taken pride in perfecting their execution of Beethoven's music. Today, recordings of his work are universally popular. For instance, 30 different recordings of the Fifth Symphony *exist, made by famous conductors and equally famous orchestras.*

"WHAT JOY IN WANDERING THROUGH THE MEADOWS!"

Beethoven had always loved nature, and never forgot the long walks taken with his boyhood friends along the Rhine. Nature inspired many of his musical themes. The *Pastoral Symphony* is a hymn to the countryside and the joys it inspires in man's heart. Some of his friends remembered him walking alone in the fields and through the woods, wrapped in his blue frock coat, his hands behind his back and a white scarf around his neck. While walking, he talked and sang to himself. Sometimes he stopped and, seating himself under a tree, took from his pocket a notebook and a pen. He wrote, now thoughts, now musical notations. In his last years, the countryside granted him only the soothing view of its landscape; for the great man, silence had descended on all things.

Beethoven found consolation in nature from physical and moral distress, from disappointments and bitterness. He had come to the point of admitting, "I love a tree more than a man; woods and rocks furnish the answer one expects." To Thérèse Malfatti he once wrote, "I have fun like a child. What joy in wandering through the meadows, among trees and flowers. It seems to me impossible that anyone can love nature as I do." Vienna, gloomy on rainy days, became for him sheer torture when the wind blew. Then he felt the overpowering desire to live in the woods. Above: Beethoven in the valley of Nussdorf. Right: one of the folk dances the Maestro enjoyed.

On a summer day, Beethoven was chatting with his pupil Ferdinand Ries on a quiet country road, when the muted sound of a bagpipe was heard in the distance. Ries said, "Maestro, listen to this beautiful sound." Beethoven listened intently, but the countryside was, for him, tragically silent. Ries understood and added quickly, "The shepherd has stopped playing." Beethoven shook his head and said nothing. His countenance suffused with sadness, he returned home and shut himself silent and alone in his room. Above: the country around Bonn where Beethoven liked to walk, before moving to Vienna. Left: the Maestro improvises at the house of the shoemaker Franz.

BEETHOVEN AND GOETHE

Once, during their stay in Teplitz, Beethoven and Goethe were walking along a boulevard when they saw approaching, in a coach, the entire Imperial family. Goethe uncovered his head, moved aside and bowed as etiquette prescribed. Beethoven, instead, pressed his hat down over his eyes, buttoned up his overcoat and stared proudly ahead. In spite of his attitude, the Empress greeted him first, and the Archduke took off his hat. Beethoven later told Goethe with satisfaction, "Those people know me." About this episode he once commented, "When someone like myself and Goethe are together, those gentlemen should feel our greatness." Goethe was too much a man of the world to assume such an unorthodox attitude. Above: the Eger gate, from a drawing by Goethe. Left: three portraits of Goethe of which the first is by F. Jagemann. On the right page: the young Goethe skating.

Even before meeting him, Beethoven greatly admired the poet Wolfgang Goethe. He wrote the *Egmont* overture, "only for love of his poems that bring me happiness." Between 1810 and 1812 he also set to music a few "lieder" based on Goethe's poems. The two great men met in Teplitz in 1812 through their common friend, Bettina von Brentano. However, the difference in temperament made a deep friendship impossible between the impetuous Beethoven and the refined and diplomatic Goethe. From their respective journals and from letters written to friends, we can deduce that their relationship was one of polite tolerance. When they met, Beethoven was 41 and Goethe 62. Once, as they took a walk together, Goethe showed his annoyance at the number of people who bowed as they passed. "Your excellency should not worry," commented Beethoven with an ironical smile. "Perhaps these bows are directed only at me." On one occasion Beethoven played for Goethe. The poet spoke of this experience to the critic Zelter: "His talent amazed me. Unfortunately, he is an utterly untamed personality, but he is not altogether wrong in finding the world detestable. Because of his personality, he cannot bring happiness either to himself or to others. He is to be excused and pitied, though, because his hearing is weakening. This is perhaps more damaging to his contacts with society than to his art. Reserved by nature, he becomes even more so because of his infirmity."

Goethe never mentioned Beethoven in his writings. He probably feared him, as he must have feared the effects of his stormy music over that peace of mind he had acquired at the price of so much self-denial. Mendelssohn, who met the 80-year-old poet at Weimar, related that Goethe did not like to hear people speak of Beethoven. Nevertheless, he listened one day to the first movement of the *Fifth Symphony*. The dramatic overture deeply troubled him; yet he feigned composure and only commented, "It is sublime music but, at the same time, bereft of reason. One would think that the concert hall is about to give way." But he went home pale and, at dinner, spoke to no one. Thereafter he no longer listened to Beethoven's music.

"HE TOO IS A MAN LIKE ALL OTHERS"

Beethoven had been a republican since his student days at the University of Bonn. The French Revolution had fascinated him. He had once jotted down in his notebook the prediction, "In fifty years, all republics will be formed." In Vienna, as an artist patronized by princes, he was able to observe, at close range, the inefficiency of government and aristocracy. He condemned them as obstacles to freedom of thought, and disliked equally imperialists and clerics. When he saw his political dream begin to materialize in the birth of the French Republic, Napoleon became to him a symbol of the high ideals of liberty, justice and brotherhood. Napoleon, as Consul, was to inspire his *Third Symphony*. On its cover he wrote with his own hand, "Bonaparte." However, shortly before the composition was performed, news reached him that Napoleon had proclaimed himself Emperor. Beethoven condemned this seizure of power. Upon learning of his imminent coronation, he uttered angrily, "Then he too is a man like all others! He too shall trample upon our rights and fulfill only his ambition!" In a fit of rage, he approached the table on which the score of "Bonaparte" was placed, and ripped its cover. With his own hand he wrote this new title: "Heroic Symphony to Celebrate the Memory of a Great Man."

The fall of Napoleon in 1814 led to the Congress of Vienna. Its purpose was to solve all the political and territorial disputes of Europe after the French invasions. To Vienna came the Czar of Russia, the kings of Denmark, Prussia, Bavaria, and Württemberg, with their princes, ministers, diplomats and court ladies. To entertain the distinguished guests, the Austrian Emperor organized a series of magnificent festivities. It was said at the time that the members of the Congress danced more than they worked. During a reception at the Rasoumowsky palace, Beethoven was introduced to all the aristocracy of Europe, and crowned heads bowed to the great composer.

Beethoven pitied Napoleon for his tragic end, a consequence of his unbounded ambition. He fully agreed with the ideas presented by the congress and the readjustments effected. On the left page, top: the meeting of the Austrian Emperor with the King of Prussia and the Russian Czar during the Congress of Vienna. Below: military parade at the Prater on October 18, 1814. On this page, above: masked ball in honor of the members of the congress. Left: carrousel of the imperial riding school. Beethoven personally sent an invitation to all the monarchs present at the congress for a concert at the Rasoumowsky palace. It was a memorable evening. The Maestro directed the cantata, The Glorious Moment, Wellington's Victory, *and the* Seventh Symphony. *Prince Rasoumowsky, who usually had a stern and almost malevolent countenance, was seen weeping that evening for the enthusiastic and warm tribute paid to Beethoven by the princes of Europe. A second concert, held at the palace of Archduke Rudolph, had similar success. About 6,000 people were present, and the press unanimously defined the evening as "triumphal."*

AN UNGRATEFUL NEPHEW

Johann and Karl van Beethoven did not resemble their brother Ludwig. In Vienna, where the Maestro had invited them to stay so that the family could be together, they returned his attentions with scorn. Karl ridiculed him in front of his friends, and even sold his music secretly. Yet the malicious, shrill-voiced Johann was even worse. An apothecary, after doing a profitable business in army supplies, he retired to a castle in the country. Once he sent a note of greeting to Ludwig, signing himself, "Johann van Beethoven, Landowner." Ludwig returned the note after writing on the back, "Ludwig van Beethoven, 'Brainowner.'" At his death in 1815, Karl left a nine-year-old son. In his will he wrote, "I am trustful that Ludwig shall have for my son the same friendship and affection he has so often shown to me." This last wish was sacred to Beethoven. He became the guardian of his nephew Karl, and sent him off to a good boarding school. However, the boy's mother demanded custody of her son in a court of law. According to the law, the guardian had to prove that he was of noble birth. It is reported that, at this request, Beethoven placed his index finger first on his forehead, then on his heart, saying to the judges, "Here is the proof of my noble rank." Finally, on April 18, 1820, after many appeals, the court granted Beethoven full custody of the boy.

Beethoven was a second father to Karl. He lavished on him his time, affection and money. But Karl was deceitful, spoiled and unruly. While his uncle had him study music and spared no expense for his upbringing, the youth was cold and contemptuous toward him. He associated with the wrong friends and was ashamed of the composer's deafness. Once he even ran away from home. Nevertheless, Beethoven, who had always longed for a family and a son of his own, forgave him everything. Failing his exams, Karl bought a gun and, climbing a hill near Baden, tried to shoot himself. He succeeded only in wounding himself superficially. Hearing of the attempted suicide, Beethoven was dismayed. He had a fit of anger. He cried. But, in the end, he rushed to the bedside of his "son." Karl finally decided to change his ways, and embraced a military career.

Beethoven's two brothers did not lead a happy married life. Karl married a disreputable woman who spent long hours in inns of ill repute, drinking and smoking. Johann married his housekeeper, a plump woman without scruples who brought him a daughter as a wedding gift. Beethoven nicknamed his two sisters-in-law, respectively, "the queen of the night" and "the lump." Obviously he had no great liking for them. On the left page: the Hauptplatz in Linz where Johann van Beethoven had his apothecary shop. On this page, above: portraits of Johann and of his nephew Karl. Below: an affectionate letter sent by Beethoven to his nephew.

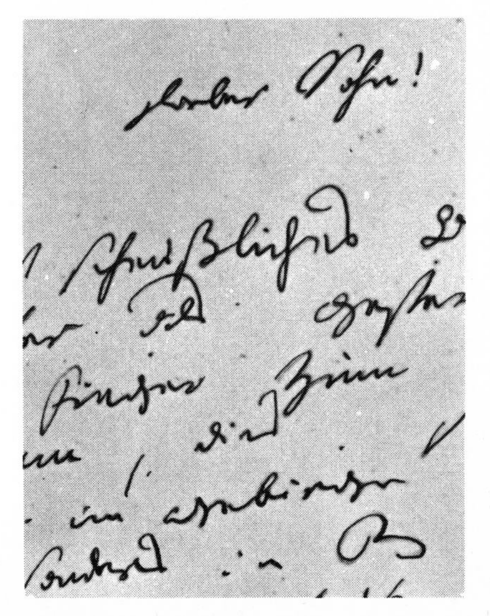

BEETHOVEN AND HIS CONTEMPORARIES

Cherubini, whose portrait we see above, held Beethoven in such high esteem that, in Paris, he became a confirmed advertiser of his works. Beethoven considered him "the greatest of all living composers." Beethoven never became very friendly with Schubert (above, right, playing for a group of friends, and on the right page during a soirée in a private home in Vienna), although they met often in restaurants, music shops and at concerts. With Weber, things were different. We reproduce here (above) his meeting with the Maestro at Mödling. His encounters with Rossini (right) and with Liszt (on the right page) were casual.

Because of his difficult personality, Beethoven did not make lasting friendships among the great musicians of his times. He met briefly Cherubini, Weber, Liszt, Rossini and Schubert. He had a closer acquaintance with Mozart, Haydn and Salieri, but only because they had been his teachers.

In April, 1822, Gioachino Rossini came to Vienna with the Italian opera company. A publisher brought him to visit Beethoven. The two entered unnoticed the studio where the Maestro was working. When, raising his eyes, he noticed his visitors, he immediately recognized the young Rossini and greeted him warmly: "Rossini, the composer of the 'Barbiere'! I congratulate you, dear Rossini; it is an excellent work. I read it with great delight." Rossini, moved, took hold of Beethoven's hand, exclaiming, "Maestro, you are a genius!" Beethoven did not hear. Only when Rossini had repeated the compliment did he answer, speaking in Italian, "Rossini, I am a very unhappy man . . . only an unhappy man. . . ."

In 1823, Karl Maria von Weber, who had conducted

the *Fidelio* in Dresden with great success, went to Baden to meet Beethoven. He described him later as gray-haired and disheveled, with a forehead "as high as a temple," and small eyes under bushy eyebrows. Beethoven's first words to him were, "Ah, it is you, you rascal! Greetings!" Of that meeting, Weber reported, "We spent the afternoon together, cheerfully.... At the table this boorish man literally courted me, as if I had been a lady." When they parted, Beethoven embraced him and held his hand for a long while. Finally he promised, "If I can, I will come to the premiere of your 'Euryanthe.'"

The 11-year-old Liszt was introduced to Beethoven by Karl Czerny. Ludwig looked him over and then made him play a fugue by Bach. When he had finished, he asked him to play the same piece again but on a different tonality. At the end of the audition Beethoven caressed him, repeating to himself, "The little devil!" Before letting him go, he kissed him on the forehead, saying, "You shall make many men happy. There is nothing better than that."

"LET IT FLOW FROM MY HEART TO THE HEART OF ALL MEN"

For years Beethoven worked on his *Missa Solemnis*. It was ready in 1822. He planned to have it performed at the installation of the Archduke Rudolph as Archbishop of Olmütz. More than music inspired by a religious ceremony, the *Missa* was a declaration of personal faith. To those who saw him at work on the *Missa*, Beethoven seemed a person possessed. Dripping with sweat, he marked the tempo with hands and feet and, pounding on the piano, disturbed all the neighbors. Finally, as he listened to what he had written, the creative fury subsided. To the "Kyrie Eleison" he wrote the heading, "Let it flow from my heart to the heart of all men." The composition of the *Missa Solemnis* marked a deepening of his faith in God.

The *Missa Solemnis* was not published until 1826. At first the publishers hesitated to print it because they feared that the public would not receive it well. Besides, Beethoven wanted a generous reward for his work. He was sure that the *Missa* had great artistic value. Also, now that his health was growing worse, he wanted to draw some profit from it to provide for Karl's future. The *Missa* was offered to the courts of Europe, but without success. Louis XVIII awarded Beethoven a gold medal. The King of Prussia sent him a diamond ring that on its journey to Vienna was replaced by a worthless one. Only in April, 1824, did the Russian Czar have the *Missa Solemnis* performed. Subsequently, a publisher in Mainz acquired it for 100 florins.

In 1820, returning to Vienna after an invigorating vacation at Baden, Beethoven agreed to conduct the *Fidelio* at the Kartner Theater. However, because of his deafness, such confusion ensued between orchestra and choir that the performance almost met with complete failure. Anxiety and pity spread among the audience, and the Maestro could only look around in dismay. At the end of the first act, the director of the theater sent him a note on which he had written, "I beg you not to continue." After reading this, Beethoven remained silent for a time, his head bent. Then he turned suddenly and left the theater, walking quickly home. Once there, he threw himself on the couch, hiding his face in his hands. In that attitude he remained deep into the night. But he was to realize that joy could also be reached through grief. It is this enduring message that his music transmits to humanity.

While the Viennese believed that Beethoven's creative power had exhausted itself, he worked on his last sonatas and on the Missa Solemnis. *A few years before his death, he wrote to his friend Bettina von Brentano, "If my income were not inadequate to my needs, I would only compose symphonies, church music and perhaps a few quartets." In Baden, where he used to go for treatment and rest, he would sit under the ancient trees to meditate and compose. In front of him stretched sloping hills and wide meadows. As he wrote, he would beat the tempo of his compositions with his hand on the grass. In 1820 the Viennese authorities granted him honorary citizenship. On the left page, center: a view of Baden, a health resort with hot springs. Above: the valley of Helena, near Baden, in Beethoven's time. On this page, below: a view of the stream that flows into the valley.*

THE TRIUMPHANT NINTH

Although ill and worried about his nephew, Beethoven found the strength to compose his most monumental work. Beethoven was searching for a goal that would transcend the world of man, and he proposed to express it through a new symphony. Its last movement inspired by Schiller's "Ode to Joy," the *Ninth Symphony* was begun in 1817, although its final draft was completed only in 1824. If the *Missa Solemnis* had risen above human limitation, the *Ninth Symphony* turned to humanity, pointing to the path of a newly discovered truth: the brotherhood of man and, through it, the attainment of supreme joy.

The Viennese believed that Beethoven's musical inspiration was exhausted. However, when word spread that he had composed a new symphony, he was urged to have it performed as soon as possible. Foreign opera predominated at the time, and it was thought that the work of a native composer would counterbalance its rapid diffusion. Beethoven agreed to have a part of the *Missa Solemnis* and the entire *Ninth Symphony* performed in Vienna. Yet what message could a deaf musician entrust to humanity after so many years of silence? The Viennese waited expectantly for the answer.

The negotiations concerning the performance were long. There were obstacles in finding a hall, a conductor, a choir and a sponsor. Moreover, the Hapsburg censorship forbade the performance of the *Missa Solemnis* in a secular hall. Finally, on May 7, 1824, the performance took place under the direction of Schuppanzigh in a hall overflowing with people. Beethoven, seated in the orchestra, his back turned to the audience, heard nothing, not even the great ovation at the end. One of the singers had to take him by the hand and turn him toward the public so that he could see the riot of appreciation. The Maestro bowed. When he lifted his head, his eyes were full of tears. When it was all over, he fainted.

Mödling was a romantic village near Vienna. It is still famous because, in its peaceful surroundings, Beethoven composed the Missa Solemnis *and the* Ninth Symphony. *These two masterpieces met with immediate success. However, they did not bring much money to their composer. After the success of the* Ninth, *Vienna no longer held concerts of his music. He sadly commented in his journal, "The most important thing for the aristocracy is the dance. In Vienna, people take interest only in dancers and horses."*

On the left page: a view of Mödling and (below) the house where Beethoven lived during his stay at the village. On this page, left: Friedrich Schiller, the poet of "Ode to Joy," and Frederick William III, King of Prussia, to whom the Maestro dedicated his last symphony. Below: music page with the finale of the Ninth Symphony.

All of Vienna took part in Beethoven's funeral (below, from a painting by Franz Stoeber). Eight orchestra conductors served as pallbearers. The funeral oration was written by the poet Grillparzer and read by the actor Eric Auschütz in the cemetery at Währing. Schools were closed that day, and soldiers were present to maintain order.

HE STRETCHED OUT HIS HAND TO THE SKY

For Beethoven, the year 1825 was marked by distress, illness and work, and a last change of residence. He moved to the Schwarzspanierhaus, a large convent built two centuries earlier by Spanish monks. From his windows he enjoyed a superb view of gardens, fortification walls and churches. Although suffering from gout and weak eyesight, Beethoven was planning a tenth symphony. He continued receiving requests for new music, and was pleased that people thought of him as still able to work. He spent a lot of time at home, much of it in bed. His brother Johann invited him to his estate at Gneiwendorf, but demanded to be paid for a damp little room and food inappropriate to a sick man. In the country he worked on his last quartets for strings, opus 130 and 135, and made a first score for the Tenth Symphony and the *Requiem*. With these works, he planned to inaugurate a new phase in his music.

In December, 1826, Beethoven left the inhospitable home of his brother. Although he owned a horse-drawn carriage, Johann sent his brother off on the milk cart. Feverish when he arrived in Vienna, he sent Karl for a doctor. But the young man passed on the request to a servant, and went to play billiards instead. The doctor arrived after three days. The diagnosis was pneumonia. Beethoven recovered, but liver and intestinal pains began to afflict him. His feet became swollen with dropsy. He was operated on but without success. Friends sent him choice foods and wines. He had lost weight and seemed taller than he had been. His hair, long and thick, fell in disorder over his forehead. Soon his strength left him permanently.

On March 24, 1827, he signed the *Quartet for Strings*, opus 131. Then he asked for the last rites and dozed off. On the afternoon of March 26, Beethoven, stretched out on his bed, was alone in his room. Anselm Hüttenbrenner, a pianist from Graz and friend of Schubert, arrived. He knelt near the dying man. Suddenly a raging storm broke out on the city, and the sky, rent by violent lightning, turned pitch-black. Beethoven raised his arm and stretched out his hand to the sky. Then he fell back motionless.

After Beethoven's death, his friends collected with reverence the objects that had been his silent companions in life. The house where he was born became a museum in which these relics were gathered. The most important objects in this collection are the pianos used by the Maestro. Each one of them has a story; the one bought for him by Prince Lichnowsky in 1803 (below, on the left) failed to please him because of a certain lack in sonority. His favorite piano was the Broadwood (drawing below, on the right), a sturdy and powerful instrument with perfect action.

Of Beethoven, Richard Wagner wrote, "The aim of true music remains the expression of the essence of things. To penetrate to the very bottom the intimate essence of things, almost to let a light shine forth from the things penetrated—namely, to reveal in their secret meaning so many passions of the human heart and so many of nature's marvels—this was the aim of our great Beethoven and his work. He remains for us the prototype of all musicians. Essentially, Beethoven was and remained a composer of sonatas because, in most of his instrumental compositions, the structure of the sonata was a means to explore the world of sound, and to express that stubborn personality that permitted him to remain, all his life, in a state of complete independence. His marvelous way of hearing, supported by great courage, inspired him at all times with contempt for the frivolous demands of the world, so inclined to mere pleasantness in music. In fact, he was to defend a treasure of enormous wealth from the snares of effeminate taste. Above and beyond those structures by which music still manifested itself as an agreeable art, he came to announce and express the new word, destined to interpret the profound meaning of things in this world."

1770—December 16, born in Bonn to Johann, tenor and violinist of the Elector of Saxony, and Magdalena Kewerich.

1778—May 26, gives his first recital.

1780—Pupil of Neefe.

1783—Replaces Neefe at the court. Publishes a sonata, two pieces from Bossless anthology, a fugue and a rondo.

1784—Composes a rondo and a piano concerto.

1785—Composes three quartets.

1787—March, departure from Bonn. April 7, arrives in Vienna, where he meets Mozart. Returns to Bonn to see his ailing mother. July 17, death of his mother.

1789—May 14, enrolls at the University of Bonn.

1790—Composes two cantatas for the Emperor's death and music for a ballet.

1791—Writes a few pieces for a violin concerto. December 5, death of Mozart.

1792—Composes a trio for strings. November 2–3, departure for Vienna where he arrives on November 10. Death of his father.

1793—Studies with Haydn.

1794—First symptoms of deafness. Composes the Trio for Pf., op. 1. March 29, his first performance at the Burgtheater.

1796—February–June, trip to Nuremberg, Prague, Dresden, and Berlin. In Berlin, composes the Sonata for Violoncello, op. 5. Composes the Sonata for Pf., op. 2.

1797—Composes the Sonata for Pf., op. 7, and the "Austrian War Song."

1798—Composes the Sonata for Pf., op.10, and the Sonata for Violin, op. 12. Death of Neefe.

1799—Composes the First Symphony, the Sonatas op. 13 ("Pathétique"), op. 14, and op. 49/1.

1800—Composes the Quartet for Strings, op. 18, the Septet, op. 20, the Piano Concerto, op. 37, the Ballet, "The Men of Prometheus," op. 43.

1801—Composes the "Spring" Sonata, op. 24, and the Sonata for Pf., op. 28 ("Pastoral"). Giulietta Guicciardi becomes his pupil.

1802—October 6 and 10, writes the "Testament of Heiligenstadt." Composes the Variations on the "Eroica," the Sonata op. 27 ("Moonlight"), the Second Symphony, op. 36.

1803—Works on the "Eroica." Completes and performs the Piano Concerto op. 37 (on April 5), the "Kreutzer" Sonata, "The Mount of Olives," and the Songs of Gellert.

1804—Composes the "Waldstein" Sonata, op. 53, the "Appassionata," op. 57, and an Andante for Pf.

1805—April 7, first public performance of the "Eroica." Composes the Piano Concerto No. 4, op. 58. Overtures Nos. 1 and 2, for "Leonore."

1806—Composes the Overture No. 3 for "Leonore," the Fourth Symphony, op. 60, the Violin Concerto, the "Rasoumowsky" Quartet, op. 59.

1807—First performance of the Fourth Symphony, and of the Piano Concerto No. 4 dedicated to Lobkowitz. Composes the Fifth Symphony. op. 67, the "Coriolan" Overture, the Missa, with premiere on September 13 at Eisenstadt.

1808—Composes the Fantasy for Piano, Chorus, and Orchestra, op. 80. Completes Sixth ("Pastoral") Symphony.

1809—May 13, bombardment of Vienna. Completes the Piano Concerto No. 5, op. 73, the Quartet, op. 74, the Sonatas for Pf., op. 78, 79, 81, the song "Mignon."

1810—May, meets Bettina Brentano. Sets to music Goethe's "Egmont," composes the Quartet, op. 95. Premiere of the Piano Concerto No. 5, in Leipzig.

1812—Meets Goethe. Letter to the "Immortal Beloved." Completes the Seventh and Eighth symphonies. ("Der glorreiche Augenblick").

1813—Composes the cantata "The Glorious Moment." December 8, premiere of the Seventh Symphony and of "Wellington's Victory."

1814—November 29, concert at Vienna's Ridotto Room, for the Congress. Composes the Sonata for Pf., op. 90.

1815—Composes the Scottish Songs, op. 108.

1816—Composes the Sonata for Pf., op. 101, and the Six Songs for "An die Ferne Geliebte."

1817—First score of the Ninth Symphony.

1818—Composes the "Hammer-Klavier Sonata."

1820—Composes the Sonata op. 109.

1822—Composes the Sonatas for Pf., op. 110 and 111. Completes the "Missa Solemnis." Composes the Overture to "Die Weihe des Hauses," op. 124.

1824—Completes the Ninth Symphony, composes the Variations, op. 120 and the Diabelli Variations. February 8, letter to Goethe. April 6, premiere of the "Missa Solemnis" for Archduke Rudolph.

1825—Premiere of the Quartet op. 127 in Vienna in March. Composes the Quartets op. 130 and 132, and Grand Fugue, op. 133.

1826—Composes the Quartets op. 131 and 135. December, falls ill of pneumonia.

1827—January 3, draws up his will. March 24, his illness grows worse and he receives the last rites. March 26, dies at 5:45 P.M.

The reproductions in this volume are found in the following collections: Berlin, Nationalgalerie, p. 27. Bologna, Museo Bibliografico Musicale, p. 42. Bonn, Beethovenhaus, pp. 4, 6, 7, 8, 27, 33, 43, 44, 52, 72-73, 74; Stadtarchiv, p. 8. Genf, Bibliothèque Publique et Universitaire, p. 66. Graz, Lichnowsky Collection, p. 26. Lahr, Gleichstein Collection, p. 27. Malines, Archives, p. 4. Milan, Museo della Scala, title page, pp. 44-45, 48, 66. Paris, S. de Breuning Collection, p. 52; Bibliothèque Nationale, p. 37; Bibliothèque du Conservatoire, p. 52; Vienna, Association of Friends of Music, pp. 16, 26, 33, 37; Artaria Archives, p. 39; Haslinger Archives, p. 39; Historisches Museum der Stadt, pp. 16, 20, 21, 25, 27, 28, 28-29, 34, 35, 36, 37, 38, 41, 46, 47, 50, 50-51, 51, 52, 53, 54-55, 67, 68, 70, 74; Kunsthistorisches Museum, pp. 12-13, 15, 26, 26-27; Streicher Collection, p. 52; Nationalbibliothek, pp. 19, 22, 24, 26, 27, 30, 33, 35, 36, 37, 39, 46, 47, 52, 26, 57, 65, 66. Weimar, Goethe National Museum, pp. 56, 60. Wiesbaden, Private Collection, p. 52. Zurich, R. Bory Collection, p. 67; Bodmer Collection, pp. 33, 58. Photographic credits, P. Brassine, p. 4. Bruckmann Verlag, p. 32. F. Falchieri and G. Doli, p. 42. Marzari, title page, pp. 44-45, 48, 66. Meyer, pp. 12-13, 15, 16, 17, 20-21, 25, 26-27, 28, 29, 34, 35, 36, 38, 41, 50, 50-51, 51, 53, 54-55, 63, 67, 68, 70. Sachsse, pp. 6, 72-73. Ullstein Bilderdienst, p. 49, and Photographic Archives of Mondadori.

GROSSE SONATE
für das
Hammer-Klavier.
Seiner Kais. Königl. Hoheit und Eminenz,
dem Durchlauchtigsten Hochwürdigsten
HERRN HERRN ERZHERZOG
RUDOLPH von OESTERREICH
Cardinal und Erzbischoff von Olmütz
in tiefster Ehrfurcht gewidmet
von
Ludwig van Beethoven.
WIEN, bey ARTARIA und COMP.

OUVERTURE
à grand orchestre
à SON ALTESSE MONSEIGNEUR LE PRINCE
Nicolas de Galitzin
par
LOUIS v. BEETHOVEN.
Oeuvre 124.

pour
Violon, Alto, Clarinette, Corne, Basson,
Violoncelle et Contre-Basse
à Sa Majesté
MARIE THERESE
L'Impératrice romaine
LOUIS VAN BEETHOVEN.

Christus am Oelberge
Oratorium
Musik von
L. v. Beethoven.
Klavierauszug.

GRANDE SONATE
pour le
Piano Forte
composée et dédiée
à Monsieur le Comte de Browne
par
LOUIS van BEETHOVEN.
Oeuvre XXII.

SONATE
pour le
Forte - Piano
avec un Violoncelle
composée et dédiée
à Madame la Baronne de Braun
par
LOUIS VAN BEETHOVEN.

SONATES
pour le
Piano Forte
avec un VIOLON
composées et dédiées
A Monsieur le Comte Maurice de Fries
par
LOUIS VAN BEETHOVEN.

Die Ruinen von Athen.
Ein Nachspiel
mit Chören und Gesängen.
Zur Eröffnung des neuen Theaters
in Pesth
verfaßt
von
August von Kotzebue.
In Musik gesetzt
von
Ludwig van Beethoven.
Aufgeführt den 9. Febr. 1812.
Pesth 1812.

POLONOISE
pour le
Piano-Forte
composée et dédiée
à S. M.
Elisabetha Alexiewna
IMPÉRATRICE DE TOUTES LES RUSSIES
par
LOUIS VAN BEETHOVEN

ENTR'ACTES
à grand Orchestre
L. v. Beethoven.
à Leipzic

Grosse Sinfonie
LUDWIG VAN BEETHOVEN
Vollständige Partitur.

TROIS SONATES
pour le Pianoforte
avec l'accompagnement d'un Violon,
composées et dédiées
à Sa Majesté
ALEXANDRE I.
Empereur de toutes les Russies
par
LOUIS van BEETHOVEN.
Oeuvre XXX.

Messa
à quattro Voci coll' accompagn.to dell' Orchestra
LUIGI VAN BEETHOVEN
Drey Hymnen
für vier Singstimmen mit Begleitung des Orchesters
Sr Durchl. dem Herrn Fürsten von Kinsky
Louis v. Beethoven.

Neue Oper.
Fidelio,
oder:
Die eheliche Liebe.
Eine Oper in 3 Akten
Die Musik ist von Ludwig van Beethoven.

SONATA
per il Piano-forte ed un Violino obligato
scritta in uno stilo molto concertante,
quasi come d'un concerto.
Composta e dedicata al suo amico
R. KREUZER
L. van BEETHOVEN.
Opera 47.

Herr Ludwig van Beethoven
eine große musikalische Akademie